8.50

D1233495

EFFECTIVE TEACHING METHODS FOR AUTISTIC CHILDREN

Effective Teaching Methods for Autistic Children

By

ROSALIND C. OPPENHEIM, M.A.

Director, The Rimland School for Autistic Children
Evanston, Illinois

With a Foreword by

Bernard Rimland, Ph.D.

Institute for Child Behavior Research
San Diego, California

CHARLES C THOMAS • PUBLISHER
Springfield • Illinois • U. S. A.

Published and Distributed Throughout the World by
CHARLES C THOMAS • PUBLISHER
Bannerstone House
301–327 East Lawrence Avenue, Springfield, Illinois, U.S.A.

© *1974, by* CHARLES C THOMAS • PUBLISHER
ISBN 0-398-02858-3

Library of Congress Catalog Card Number: 74 4116

*With THOMAS BOOKS careful attention is given to all details of
manufacturing and design. It is the Publisher's desire to present
books that are satisfactory as to their physical qualities and artistic
possibilities and appropriate for their particular use. THOMAS
BOOKS will be true to those laws of quality that assure a good
name and good will.*

Printed in the United States of America
CC-11

Library of Congress Cataloging in Publication Data

Oppenheim, Rosalind C
  Effective teaching methods for autistic children.

  Bibliography: p.
  1. Autism. 2. Mentally handicapped children—Education. I. Title.
[DNLM: 1. Autism—In infancy and childhood. 2. Education, Special.
3. Teaching. LC4661 062e 1973]
LC4580.066   371.9'2   74-4116
ISBN 0-398-02858-3

To my autistic son, Ethan,
and to all the Ethans everywhere:
May the future bring them some measure
of happiness and fulfillment

52227

FOREWORD

Mrs. Oppenheim entered the teaching profession by necessity. Being the mother of a severely afflicted autistic child who is now almost an adult, she discovered through bitter personal experience that such youngsters were excluded from the possible benefits of special education, because no one seemed to know how to teach them, or to cope with their bizarre behavior. She found that there was literally no school in the entire Chicago metropolitan area in which her son was acceptable. Lacking an alternative, she undertook to educate him herself. The first school was her own living room; however, as her skill and confidence grew and as her success became known to other parents in a similar plight, she quickly graduated to teaching and administering in parent-initiated schools. Feeling the need for more formal education herself, she earned a Master's Degree in special education at Northeastern Illinois University.

In *Effective Teaching Methods for Autistic Children*, Rosalind Oppenheim describes the teaching techniques she developed during her more than thirteen years in the field. However, this book is more than a mere description of techniques. It also outlines classroom approaches and child-management methods that are designed to overcome the children's resistance and behavioral difficulties, and thus facilitate the learning process.

She was not yet a professional teacher at the time she initially began to tutor her 4-year-old autistic child in 1959. About her early teaching experiences with him, she says, "When I first began, he was so resistant, so utterly disinterested and unresponsive, that I felt that I was setting out to move a mountain. But somewhere along the way, I discovered that the mountain was only *papier-mache*." Within fifteen months, her then-nonverbal son had learned to read and write at levels considerably beyond his chronological age. This was such an astounding development, particularly in the light of his atypical general functioning, that Mrs. Oppenheim felt impelled to sound a note of hope for other parents of autistic and autistic-type children. The story of her son's achievement was published in the June 17, 1961, issue of *The Saturday Evening Post*, and attracted nation-wide attention.

Now, twelve years later, she is once again sharing the professional expertise she has gained during her years of teaching such youngsters. Many of the techniques she describes are innovative and creative. Others are traditional teaching procedures, ingeniously adapted to the needs and the disabilities of autistic-type children.

The author brought with her into the teaching situation no pre-conceived notions about a ceiling on the autistic child's ability to learn. Perhaps because there were no previously established guidelines about either what or how to teach autistic children, she felt free to venture into teaching areas which no one else had previously investigated, particularly with nonverbal youngsters. Thus, for example, she advocates asking both nonverbal and verbal autistic children *why* questions for them to answer in writing, once they have attained sufficient facility with the pencil. She reasons that this may give nonverbal youngsters an opportunity to draw on a reserve of inner language and thus reveal a latent cognitive ability that they are unlikely—and perhaps unable—to demonstrate spontaneously in their general functioning. For verbal autistic children, she maintains that written expression at this cognitive level may enable them to bypass the difficulties with oral speech that may limit the extent to which they can exhibit their inner intellectual development. She does not suggest that this approach produces positive results with every autistic child; but she demonstrates that this is an area that should certainly be explored with each child.

Mrs. Oppenheim is a strong advocate of the idea that an effort should be made to teach academic readiness and then reading, writing and arithmetic to *all* autistic and autistic-type children, regardless of the abnormalities and developmental immaturities of their functioning. She maintains—and demonstrates—that the teaching of academic skills can proceed side-by-side with the teaching of social skills.

The effectiveness of the author's teaching methods is supported by the case reports in Chapter V. All seven of her pupils, even those who were still mute, achieved gains in proficiency in reading and other academic areas. In a very real sense, their progress and the cognitive abilities that these case reports reveal, epitomize the poignant enigma of autism. Apart from testifying to the importance of teaching, they are a telling argument in favor of persistent and continuing research into the causes and the cure(s) for this tragic affliction.

In the final chapter, Mrs. Oppenheim discusses a specific problem for possible research. She calls attention to an interesting anomaly that she and others have observed in some autistic children: Their seeming inability to "translate comprehension into motor performance." Further investigation into this phenomenon, she suggests, might prove productive in pinpointing the precise nature of the language deficits of at least one sub-category of autistic children. This is indeed an important and intriguing problem, although my own feeling is that it is better categorized as an intrinsic deficit in motivation, rather than in language.

The book concludes with a brief outline of some of the areas of remedial education that require much greater effort if the needs of the more-severely handicapped autistic child are to be met: development of optimal methods of vocational training; the establishment of modified sheltered workshops that are geared to the specific needs of still-severely-afflicted autistic adults; and the organization of residential communities that would provide a sheltered but productive and meaningful lifestyle for those who require it.

This book will prove valuable for both parents and professionals who are involved in the teaching of autistic children. Perhaps its most significant contribution is that it demolishes unequivocally the myth that autistic youngsters are unreachable and unteachable.

BERNARD RIMLAND, PH.D.
Institute for Child Behavior Research
San Diego, California

ACKNOWLEDGMENTS

This book makes no pretense of being the last word on the subject of teaching autistic children. In fact, it would probably be more appropriate to call it one of the first words— particularly since it is still being written even as it is being published, in the sense that the development of new and more effective methods, procedures and behavioral strategies is a continuing process.

The teaching techniques outlined here are the distillation of some thirteen years of teaching and working with autistic children. *Effective Teaching Methods for Autistic Children* is not a general textbook on teaching methods *per se*. It focuses instead on the devising of new procedures as well as on the *how* of adapting already-proven methods so that they will be effective in reaching and teaching severely afflicted nonverbal and verbal autistic and autistic-like children. Hopefully, the ideas presented here will prove useful to both professionals and parents.

Inevitably, this book reflects modifications of some of the methods and approaches that were taught to me over the years. To all of these former instructors I extend my appreciation. Two in particular merit special mention.

In the course of seeking help for my nonverbal autistic son, I was privileged to benefit from the teaching and the guidance of the late Dr. Newell C. Kephart, who was at the time of his death the Director of the Kephart Glen Haven Achievement Center in Fort Collins, Colorado. Dr. Kephart's research dealt with the need to establish perceptual-motor skills as the underlying foundation for the teaching of more complex academic skills. It was under his supervision that I initially undertook the teaching of my son, an endeavor which ultimately culminated in my becoming a professional teacher. It is impossible to adequately convey the depth of Dr. Kephart's interest and concern, and the kindness with which he helped me to apply his research findings in my teaching, during the years when my son was his patient. He had great influence on the educational philosophy that I developed. I am profoundly grateful to him.

The second acknowledgment which must be made here is to Dr. O. Ivar Lovaas of the University of California at Los Angeles. Dr. Lovaas pioneered in developing speech training methods for nonverbal autistic children. For a several-week period during the summer of 1965 and again in 1966, he and his associates very generously taught me how to apply his then-developed techniques. To him, too, I am most grateful.

There are others to whom I want to extend my thanks: Among them, the dedicated teaching staff at The Rimland School for Autistic Children, and notably my gifted colleague, head teacher Carol Ann C. Auclair, who is still refining the teaching methods outlined here and simultaneously developing innovative new procedures. It was her suggestion that I record in an organized fashion the teaching methods in use at The Rimland School that led to the writing of this book. Appreciation is also due to Dr. Glen Thompson of Northeastern Illinois University for his encouraging comments after reviewing the original manuscript of this book; to the National Society for Autistic Children, from whose publications and materials I have gained much valuable information; and to Dr. Bernard Rimland for the writings and research which have contributed so greatly to the current interest in autism.

These acknowledgments would be wanting without special mention of my indebtedness to the autistic children I have taught, who have in turn taught me so much and from whom there is still so much to be learned.

Finally, I must express my gratitude to my husband, Joe, and my son, Ethan, for their patient making-do with the fringes of my attention while I was engrossed in the writing of this book.

ROSALIND C. OPPENHEIM

CONTENTS

EFFECTIVE TEACHING METHODS
FOR AUTISTIC CHILDREN

Chapter I

INTRODUCTION

IN 1943, LEO KANNER, then the pre-eminent child psychiatrist in the United States, published a paper outlining in detail the case histories of eleven profoundly atypical children whose unique presenting symptoms seemed to constitute a previously unreported clinical entity. In his paper, entitled *Autistic Disturbances of Affective Contact*, Kanner (1943) described the basic similarities in the bizarre behavior and maladaptive functioning of these eleven children, whom he had seen over a period of some years at the Child Psychiatry Clinic at Johns Hopkins Hospital. The following year, he published a subsequent paper in which he named the new syndrome "early infantile autism" (Kanner, 1944).

The four cardinal symptoms or behavioral characteristics which Kanner (1943) delineated as fundamental to a diagnosis of autism were: (1) social withdrawal: "an *extreme autistic aloneness*" (p. 242) from the very beginning of life; (2) either mutism, or, when speech was present, the failure to use language "to convey meaning to others. . . . As far as the communicative functions of speech are concerned, there is no fundamental difference between the eight speaking and the three mute children" (p. 243); (3) "an anxiously obsessive desire for the maintenance of sameness" (p. 243) in the environment; and (4) a preoccupation with the manipulation of objects and monotonously repetitive play habits, resulting in a "severe limitation in the variety of spontaneous activity" (p. 246). Kanner was impressed by the seeming intelligence and the "strikingly intelligent physiognomies" (p. 247) of his autistic patients. Indeed, some writers include "evidence of good cognitive potentialities" (Moore and Shiek, 1971, p. 451) as the fifth cardinal symptom of autism.

In the years since the publication of Kanner's original papers, numerous other clinicians and researchers have confirmed

3

his findings. However, in the more recent literature, some workers (Rutter, 1966a and 1966b; Rutter, 1968; Rutter and Bartak, 1971; Wing and Wing, 1971; Lorna Wing, 1972) have disagreed with Kanner's contention (1943; 1957) that children afflicted with early infantile autism "are all unquestionably endowed" (p. 247) with the potential for basically normal intelligence. These writers maintain that some autistic children have an IQ which is within the normal range, while others are, in fact, mentally deficient.

The incidence of autism is relatively rare: approximately two to five cases per 10,000 population—as contrasted with a prevalence of forty cases of severe mental subnormality per ten thousand population (Wing, 1966). The sex ratio is approximately four boys to one girl (Rimland, 1964). According to Rimland (1964), approximately "half of all autistic children" fail to develop speech (p. 15).

Of Kanner's original eleven cases, three were nonverbal and have remained mute into adulthood (Kanner, 1971):

Kanner's Case 3, Richard M., was placed in a state school for exceptional children at the age of eight and one-half. Subsesequently, the institution reported, "We accepted him as essentially a custodial problem . . . ." (p. 125). At age 33, Richard, still institutionalized, takes care of his personal needs, and responds to his name and simple conmands. "He continues to be withdrawn and cannot be involved in any structured activities" (p. 126).

Virginia S., Kanner's Case 6, has resided in a state institution since she was five years old. A psychological report written when Virginia was seven says she "pays no attention to what is said to her but quickly comprehends whatever is expected. Her performance reflects discrimination, care, and precision." She achieved an IQ of 94 with the nonlanguage test items. "Without a doubt, her intelligence is superior to this . . . She is mostly self-sufficient and independent . . . finds pleasure in dealing with things, about which she shows imagination and initiative" (p. 129). In 1970, at age 39, Virginia handled her basic needs, but had to be reminded to do so. She was assigned to a home economics program, where she learned to iron clothes. The 1970 report adds, "She . . . is able to follow instructions and directions . . . can identify colors . . . tell time . . . work jigsaw puzzles . . . She desires to keep to herself. . ." (p. 130).

The third mute child among Kanner's original eleven seems to have fared somewhat better than his two non-verbal counterparts. Placed in a foster home with a farm family when he was about seven or eight, Herbert B., Kanner's Case 7, has remained on the farm ever since. By age 13, he had "learned to cut wood, use the power mower, rake the lawn, set the table perfectly, and in his spare time work jigsaw puzzles . . . with the utmost skill." After the farmer died, his widow "opened a nursing home for elderly people. Herbert remained with her, took the old ladies out for walks, brought . . . their trays to their rooms . . ." (p. 131). At the time of this writing he was 34 years old.

Kanner's 1971 follow-up study gives no indication that these three children were ever given any sustained formal schooling. As Kanner sums it up,

> Richard M. . . . [and] Virginia S. . . . who spent most of their lives in institutional care, . . . lost their luster early after their admission. Originally fighting for their aloneness and basking in the contentment that it gave them, originally alert to unwelcome changes and, in their own way, struggling for the status quo, originally astounding the observer with their phenomenal feats of memory, they yielded readily to the un-interrupted self-isolation and soon settled down in a life not too remote from a nirvana-like existence. If at all responsive to psychological testing, their IQ's dropped down to figures usually referred to as low-grade moron or imbecile.
>
> This fortunately did not happen to the remaining . . . [child]. Herbert B. . . ., still mute, has not attained a mode of living that one can be jubilant about but has reached a state of limited but positive usefulness. He was placed on a farm, where, following the farmer around on his chores, he learned to participate in some of them. When the farmer died and the widow established a nursing home for elderly people, he learned to perform the functions of a kind, helpful, competent orderly, using his routine-consciousness in a goal-directed, dependable manner.

. . . One cannot help but gain the impression that State Hospital admission was tantamount to a life sentence, with evanescence of the astounding facts of rote memory, abandonment of the earlier pathological yet active struggle for the maintenance of sameness, and loss of the interest in objects added to the basically poor relation to people—in other words, a total retreat to near-nothingness. . . . (Kanner, 1971, pp. 143–144).

The early literature on the subject of autistic children is virtually devoid of descriptions of effective teaching methods. It was generally believed that autistic children, especially non-verbal autistic children, were so inaccessible that they were unreachable and unteachable.

In the main, it appears that no attempt was made to teach these children. Almost universally, the parents of a mute autistic child were advised repeatedly by a succession of professional diagnosticians to "put him away in an institution and forget about him." Autism was classified by most clinicians as one of the childhood schizophrenias; and autistic youngsters who had never developed speech were considered the most severely afflicted of all mentally ill children. Most schools, both public and private, rejected these children as uneducable (Fenichel *et al.*, 1960).

For those rare children who were fortunate enough to find their way into one of the few existent private schools, "schooling" consisted almost entirely of play therapy. Fenichel, Freedman and Klapper (1960) in a paper presented at the 1958 Annual Meeting of the American Orthopsychiatric Association, wrote, "Much of the work of the League School centers around efforts at play activities" (p. 136).*

The general assumption was that early infantile autism is psychogenic in origin. Says Carl Fenichel (1966),

Nearly every professional worker accepted the prevailing theory that "disturbed children were made disturbed by the mishandling of disturbed or inadequate parents." . . . The psy-

---

* Copyright, the American Orthopsychiatric Association, Inc., Reproduced by permission., Fenichel, C., Freedman, A. M., and Klapper, Z.: A day school for schizophrenic children. *American Journal of Orthopsychiatry, 30*(1): 130–143, 1960.

choanalytic literature that dominated the field consisted of variations on a theme: "disturbed children had been traumatized by parents who had denied them their rightful pleasures and privileges of infancy" (p. 9).

Until well into the 1960's, the belief was almost universal that autistic children required psychiatric treatment before formal teaching could begin. As Fenichel puts it (1966), "Up to recently it was generally believed that education could do little or nothing for these children and that the medical, specifically the psychiatric, profession must assume the major or total treatment responsibility" (p. 6). In actual fact, however, almost none of these youngsters—certainly virtually no nonverbal child—was receiving any kind of professional help or therapy. Fenichel continues, "Clinics rejected them as untreatable. Private psychiatric treatment was too expensive for most families" (p. 6). In any case, mute autistic children were generally considered too inaccessible to benefit from psychiatric treatment.

The direct consequence was that the few autistic children who *were* enrolled in private schools were "treated," rather than taught. Writes Fenichel (1966):

> At the beginning we believed that our teachers should play a permissive and relatively unstructured "therapeutic" role that permitted their children the freedom to ventilate hostilities, aggressions and primitive drives until basic intra-psychic conflicts were "worked through" and resolved (p. 9).

The occasional nonconformist who embarked on a more formal educational program for autistic students entered unexplored territory where it was necessary to devise new, previously untried, teaching approaches and techniques. As recently as six years ago, Wing and Wing (1966) declared,

> There is no flourishing tradition of remedial education for autistic children, as there is for the blind and the deaf. For these conditions, the rules of special teaching are now fairly well laid down and each teacher learns exactly what to do during training. It is not necessary for them to make up the rules as they go along, as Anne Macy did with Helen Keller, and as teachers of autistic children must (pp. 189–190).

This paper will outline some of the specific techniques and methods that we developed during some 13 years of teaching and working with initially nonverbal autistic children; and describe some of the resultant changes in the children. (We have used these same methods with speaking autistic children, as well. The approach is equally suitable for verbal youngsters, with whatever modifications are indicated by the quantity of *communicative* speech the talking children use.) It is too soon to predict that the future of the children so taught will be less bleak than that of their earlier, unschooled nonverbal counterparts. But it is to be hoped that among the mute autistic children who have had the benefit of sustained periods of formal schooling, a significant percentage will lead meaningful and productive lives. In any event, regardless of the ultimate outcome for individual children, the cognitive abilities demonstrated by these tragically afflicted children, when they are given the opportunity to develop their innate capacities, should be recorded in the literature.

Chapter II

RELATED RESEARCH

R IMLAND'S BOOK *Infantile Autism* (1964) included an exhaustive survey of all of the literature then extant on the subject of autism. So it may be assumed that the references given following his comment "other autistic children write but do not speak (Arnold, 1960; Oppenheim, 1961)" (p. 13), constitute the only cases recorded in the literature at the time (1962) that Rimland's book was written.

Rimland's reference to Arnold concerns a paper that Arnold wrote in 1960 entitled "Writing Instead of Speaking," in which he discusses the case of a four-year-old child who had spontaneously taught himself to write words and phrases in block letters, and "occasionally repeated" orally "what he had written: names of television programs or commercial products, slogans, jingles, etc. which he had seen on television" (p. 157). The presenting complaint, when he "was admitted . . . for evaluation of his inability to speak [was] . . . does not try to converse; can say some words and some sentences, but not distinctly; . . ." (p. 156). The multidiscipline clinical team who examined, observed, and tested this child, diagnosed him as a case of "autistic mutism" (p. 161). In fact, however, Arnold's case is not a nonverbal autistic child, since he did talk at times, though he did not use speech for communication. Nevertheless, his precocity in writing was apparently a sufficiently rare occurrence in an autistic child who had speech but no language that Arnold saw fit at the time to record it in the literature.

The source of Rimland's reference to Oppenheim is an article by this author that was published in *The Saturday Evening Post* (Oppenheim, 1961) describing the "phenomenal" (p. 58) progress in reading, writing, spelling and arithmetic of her 6-year-old nonverbal autistic son, about whom she had been told repeatedly, less than three years earlier, that the child

9

had probably "gone as far as he can go intellectually" (p. 56). The paper describes in very general terms a home-training program instituted by Dr. Newell C. Kephart (then at Purdue University) which this author and her husband followed with their child. The article does not spell out specific procedures used with the boy, other than this description of some of the preacademic activities utilized in his training program:

> Initially Ethan's resistance to this new regime was massive. The only way I could get him to use the toys I introduced was by taking his limp little hands in my own and manipulating his fingers for him. . . .
> But slowly, slowly Ethan learned that there was an increasing variety of things that he could do by himself, besides his interminable rolling of the ball. He built block towers, worked jigsaw puzzles, blew bubbles, used a scissors. His drawings—meaningless, random crayon scribbles—were prominently displayed on our kitchen bulletin board, because Ethan smiled with pleasure when Joe admired his work in the evenings. His eyes were merry, his laughter frequent during the games and pickaback rides of our evening play period. Demonstrating his newly acquired skills for Joe's applause became a regular feature of playtime. Gradually Ethan accepted our class sessions as an integral part of the daily routine (p. 58).

The paper goes on to recount some of the details of the work pursued with the child during the subsequent year:

> So Ethan and I resumed our twice-daily class sessions. Scared but daring, I started him on pre-reading workbooks. (Duck soup for Ethan, it turned out.) On December 17, 1960, I taught him how to print his name. And suddenly, astoundingly, our miracle came to pass. Ethan could express himself on paper. At last Ethan could communicate. . . . (p. 58).

Following the publication of this article, the author was besieged by hundreds of letters from distraught parents from several continents who were seeking help; a number of professionals in the field requested permission to quote portions of the article; and it was subsequently reprinted in an anthology (Kvaraceus and Hayes, 1969).

Rimland (1964), referring further to the Oppenheim paper, continues, "The Oppenheim case, unlike that of Arnold, appeared to be able to communicate through writing." Seemingly, this phenomenon was so unprecedented in an autistic child who had no speech whatever, that Rimland goes on to say, "It is possible that Oppenheim's is not a true case of infantile autism" (pp. 13-14).

Toward the middle of the 1960's, an occasional article began to appear here and there in professional journals, describing what were, at first, isolated islands of success in teaching both nonverbal and verbal autistic children.

Thus, Hewett (1964) describes in considerable detail an educational program used with Jimmy, a hospitalized 13-year-old autistic boy who had never developed speech. The program "utilized an operant conditioning approach in an effort to teach him to read and write" (p. 613). Jimmy habitually occupied himself for extended periods of time working jigsaw puzzles. Another activity in which he engaged spontaneously was the copying of whatever alphabetical letters chanced to be printed on various toys to which he had access. "This interest in jigsaw puzzles and letters served as a clue for the educational program which was subsequently launched with Jimmy," writes Hewett (p. 613).*

Using candy gumdrops for motivation, the program evolved through a series of progressive stages of increasing complexity. At the outset, Jimmy matched concrete objects and pictures. Thus, he was shown a ball; the teacher then drew a circle, while saying, "ball"; and now Jimmy was told to draw a ball. The next stage involved Jimmy's matching the word "ball" with the picture of a ball—at first, with no other choice available; and subsequently from among a multiple choice grouping. In time, Jimmy had a sight vocabulary of fifty-five words. At this point, Jimmy was taught to classify "Things we find in a house," "Things we eat" and so on, by grouping either the appropriate pictures, or the appropriate words.

"The preceding four stages took up most of the first year

---

* Reprinted with permission of the International Reading Association and F. M. Hewett. Hewett, F. M.: Teaching reading to an autistic boy through operant conditioning. *Reading Teacher, 17,* 613–618, 1964.

of Jimmy's educational program," Hewett tells us (p. 616). But Jimmy showed considerable progress in other areas, as well: He displayed intrinsic motivation and interest in both the learning procedures and the teacher. It was no longer necessary to reward him with a gumdrop after each separate response: now, "He was given gumdrops only after completion of a task (e.g., matching six picture word cards) . . ." (p. 616). His behavior was much more controlled. He displayed an avid interest in learning more and more new words. Hewett continues,

> . . . on several occasions, he tried to describe an experience he had had over the preceding week-end by means of drawings and picture cards.
>
> A notable attempt at such communication took place one day after Jimmy had visited the zoo. He combined the zoo animals with the "mama" and "daddy" cards and pointed outside the room with various grunting noises, telling the teacher of his trip to the zoo with his mother and father (p. 616).

Hewett goes on to describe the procedures by which Jimmy was taught to write. It took Jimmy only three months to learn how to write every letter of the alphabet "on verbal cue" (p. 617); and he was then able to write any word, provided the teacher spelled it aloud for him. The next step involved teaching Jimmy the writing of simple phrases, which he was thereafter required to write in order to communicate his needs and wants. Hewett concludes,

> Currently, Jimmy's written communication repertoire is being enlarged to include appropriate phrases for many of his daily activities in the hospital, e.g., "I want pool. I want to eat. I want juice. . . ." The plan is to require his communicating in this manner before a wish will be granted.
>
> In Jimmy's case, acquisition of rudimentary reading and writing skills seemed to heighten his interest in the environment and make him more accessible to social control. On the basis of such a "breakthrough" experience with Jimmy, teaching reading and writing may offer a most promising means of furthering socialization and treatment with heretofore isolated autistic children (pp. 617–618).

The approach followed by Carl Fenichel, the Director of the League School for Seriously Disturbed Children in Brooklyn, is based on keeping the child within the family despite his severe behavior disorders, "by substituting the day treatment school and the home for the mental hospital" (Fenichel, 1966, p. 6). The program does not include psychotherapy. Says Fenichel,

> We realized that what each child needs is his own personal prescription of training and education based on a psycho-educational assessment of his unique patterns of behavior and levels of functioning. This means . . . attempting to identify, analyze and describe each child's specific skills and strengths, disabilities and deficits, lags and limitations in the many basic areas involved in the learning process, including sensory and perceptual intactness, neuro-motor development, spatial relations, body image, visual and auditory discrimination and retention, ability to use symbols, understand language and form concepts (p. 8).

Once the basic disabilities are identified, a remedial program is prescribed for each child which attempts to alleviate the disabilities, or, if they prove irremediable, to compensate for them. The teaching environment is highly structured, with a "reality-oriented" curriculum involving "living-playing-learning experiences and activities that offer continuity, stability, security and a sense of achievement" (p. 14).

Sybil Elgar (1966), who directs the Society School for Autistic Children in London, advocates an educational-treatment philosphy similar to Fenichel's, although it was developed independently. She maintains that it is possible to implement a structured learning program for autistic children which simultaneously helps them in three areas: the acquisition of educational skills; social adjustment; and emotional growth. Establishing control over the child, she argues, is a vital first step "that should be dealt with as soon as possible" after a child enters school. She writes,

> . . . No one who has had to live through a screaming session lasting many hours will underrate the temptation to give in. No one who has seen the way that the behaviour of a whole family

can revolve around the oddities of one small tyrant will doubt that events must not be allowed to take this course. The resulting "struggle for power" has been described by every author who has written realistically about the education of autistic children. Only if the teacher is firm in her own authority, confident that she is right, and secure enough in her own personality to know that she is acting in the interest of the child and out of love for him, will this particular problem be successfully solved. Once it is, constructive education can begin (Elgar, 1966, pp. 213–214).

Elgar uses a multisensory approach to the teaching of speech, language comprehension, reading, writing, and arithmetic; and utilizes Montessori materials to a considerable extent. Social skills, routines of every day living, physical education, music, and art are also stressed (Elgar, 1966, 1968).

Most nonverbal autistic children (and to a lesser extent, verbal autistic youngsters, as well) exhibit no imitative behavior of any kind, prior to educational treatment. Many clinicians believe that the impoverished behavioral repertoire of the autistic child is largely due to his failure to imitate. Hingtgen, Coulter and Churchill (1967) undertook a study to determine the effectiveness of intensive reinforcement of imitative responses in three major areas: use of the body; use of objects; and vocalizations. Imitation of body movements involved such activities as holding up one finger, clapping hands, touching parts of the body, running, jumping, et cetera. The use of objects included buttoning, line drawing, brushing teeth, cutting with a scissors, and so on. The objective of the imitative vocal responses was to lead the children from imitative mouth movements such as opening the mouth, to blowing, to "the imitation of vowel and consonant sounds with a gradual progression to words" (p. 38). According to the authors' summary of this study,

> Two mute autistic children who had not shown any significant improvement following various types of traditionally oriented therapy were isolated, individually, in a room for 21 days. During approximately six hours of daily training sessions, two to six adults used food, water, and release from physical restraint to reinforce three types of imitative responses. . . . Over 200

responses of the first two types and an imitative vocabulary of 17 to 18 sounds and 11 to 18 words were established by the end of the 21-day period. . . . Five months following the initial training period the children had progressed beyond imitative responding, and were doing such things as printing letters of the alphabet using a visual or auditory cue, cutting out figures with scissors, naming various pictures and objects, etc. The results of this study suggest that a short-term intensive imitative training period might be effective in establishing a large number of behaviors which can be used by parents, teachers, and others as the foundation for working toward a broader and more spontaneous behavioral repertoire in the autistic child (pp. 42–43).

Jensen and Womack (1967) set up a therapeutic program involving the application of operant conditioning techniques with Jerry, an autistic child who had very limited use of language. Part of a clinical ward treatment program, the objectives were: "Behaviors which we wished to encourage or increase in frequency: interactive contacts with peers, use of language and persons' names, and cooperation in group play activities" (p. 31). The program was also aimed at extinguishing, or reducing, temper tantrums, spitting, hitting people, and other undersirable behaviors. Primary reinforcers (ice cream and potato chips) were coupled with a social reinforcer in the form of praise and attention. Behavior was shaped: for example, at the outset, Jerry was given a primary reinforcer at the first indication of peer proximity. "Within several weeks, Jerry was making several daily contacts with peers involving sustained interaction sequences" (pp. 31–32). Language behavior was similarly reinforced: initially one-word responses were rewarded; later, Jerry was rewarded only for using several words, or a sentence. Temper tantrums become a rarity as a result of isolating the boy in a quiet room immediately on the onset of a tantrum, and keeping him there for at least 30 minutes. Other aggressive behaviors were also effectively reduced, by slapping Jerry on the hand, or restraining him, *immediately* following the occurrence of the behavior. The program included training the child's mother in effective behavior modification techniques in the home management of the boy. Jensen and Womack conclude,

. . . we had succeeded with this child in modifying specific behavior patterns to a considerable degree. . . . the staff responded with growing enthusiasm to the evident changes . . . and the total experience resulted in a great increase in our therapeutic team morale. Such reinforcement to the therapists working with autistic children is not to be underestimated (p. 34).*

The Edison Responsive Environment (E.R.E.) "talking typewriter" has been investigated by Goodwin and Goodwin (1969) to determine whether handicapped children would respond as favorably to it as normal children had. During a 28-month period, the E.R.E. was made available to 65 autistic children for half-hour periods one to five times weekly. The Goodwins describe their experience with one of their early autistic patients, five-year-old Robbie. Robbie's behavior was so difficult that he was already on a waiting list for state hospital placement at the time of his chance referral to the E.R.E. center in 1964. Following his initial 15-minute trial with the machine,

Robbie . . . left behind him a full page of random typing interspersed with many words, [among them] 'liquid," "final," "touch," "ivory," . . . "man." He was invited to return.
At later visits, he typed "boxed," "taped," and "warped" . . . wrote an original story paraphrased from "The Flintstones," . . . As visits continued, temper tantrums, head banging, and hyperactivity gradually diminished; personal pronouns were heard; teachers were called by their proper names; meaningful reading and writing were recognized. Visits were often stormy during the next two years, but progress was measurable and outbursts were less frequent. Robbie was excluded from school until a special class for brain-injured children was started in 1968 in his local school district. His teacher reports continuing improvement in both behavior and performance (pp. 559–560).

The Goodwins report similarly favorable results with other

autistic children, some of whom developed speech following a few months of exposure to the E.R.E.

Hewett, Mayhew, and Rabb (1967) describe an experimental reading program utilizing programmed instruction techniques and the application of learning theory to teach reading to a group of children who had been considered uneducable, among them one nonverbal autistic boy. A portion of this study involved the use with three autistic subjects of an "errorless training sequence," so-called, according to Hewett *et al.*, because "The task required of the child was extremely simple and the teacher's prompting so extensive that it was difficult for him to make errors for any period of time, hence the term 'errorless training' " (p. 40). All of the children in the study, including the autistics, learned to read. Write Hewett and his associates,

> When the possibility exists that children considered unteachable and defective might be able to attain some measure of reading proficiency and hence gain the socialization and self-image benefits inherent in such attainment, it would appear that every effort should be made to explore and develop innovative and individualized instructional programs (p. 48).*

An example of another type of innovative programming is described in a pamphlet by Doernberg, Rosen and Walker, entitled *A Home Training Program for Young Mentally Ill Children* (1968). A research project initiated by The League School, Brooklyn, in 1966, the experimental program was designed "to evaluate the effectiveness of a planned parent-professional effort on a limited part-time basis in improving the functioning" of a group of children aged three to seven who had been diagnosed, but were not "currently involved in any program of educational or psychiatric services" (p. 2). The children, randomly assigned to either the Experimental

---

* Copyright, the American Orthopsychiatric Association, Inc., Reproduced by permission., Hewett, F. M., Mayhew, D., and Rabb, E.: An experimental reading program for neurologically impaired, mentally retarded, and severely emotionally disturbed children. *American Journal of Orthopsychiatry, 37:* 35–48, 1967.

or the Control Groups, were on The League School waiting list, with an equal number of verbal and nonverbal children assigned to each group. The program consisted of 30 to 40 individual one-hour weekly training sessions for each child, with the mother present as a nonparticipating observer. Teaching was "focused in the areas of self-help, communication (speech and language), socialization, and pre-and-early academic skills" (p. 2). During these sessions, the teacher made suggestions to the parent for adaptation of her methods and materials for home use, during similar training sessions that the mother conducted daily on her own with the child at home. The mothers were also given supplemental guidance weekly by the director of the program. In addition, every other week the mothers and/or fathers of the children in the Experimental Group met with a social worker and the program director "to discuss child training and management problems, family relationships and concerns of family and community living, specifically those involving the ill child" (p. 2). The children in the Control Group remained on The League School waiting list (as did those in the Experimental Group) but received no services from the school. (However, the project covered a span of two years; and at the end of the first year, the children in the Control Group were accepted into the experimental portion of the Home Training program in a cross-over design).

When the results of the research project were evaluated, the Experimental Group children showed significant gains. They had improved in virtually every area, not only in comparison with their own initial status, but also in comparison with their Control Group counterparts. Doernberg, Rosen and Walker conclude,

> Since the thrust of this program was to develop a meaningful intervention for waiting list families and their mentally ill children and since such intervention is a pervasive need due to lack of facilities, personnel and funds in agencies serving such children, the results of the study offer exciting possibilities for further development and use of this program within the context of various kinds of non-residential services . . . in which the emphasis is education (for the parent, for the child or both) . . . to make productive the waiting list time.

. . . Since this program of a direct approach to parents has been demonstrated to be effective, the program's results must lead to serious reconsideration of certain theoretical positions regarding the etiology of childhood mental illness. . . . Results of current research increasingly indicate a relation between organic and bio-chemical abnormalities and resulting atypical behavior. Whether a child's mental illness is of psychogenic or physiological origin, the Home Training Program has been demonstrated to be useful to both child and family (pp. 36–37).

DesLauriers and Carlson (1969) hold that early infantile autism is the consequence of a form of sensory and affective deprivation, resulting from a neurophysiological imbalance "between the drive-response system (Arousal System I, the reticular formation), and the incentive-motivation system (Arousal System II, the limbic system)" (p. 354). Based on this hypothesis, they set up a research project which consisted of a training program for five autistic children aged two to five years, four of whom are described as initially lacking both expressive and receptive language. Each of the children was treated on an outpatient basis, receiving either two or three one-hour sessions of individual therapy per week. The thrust of the treatment approach was a therapeutic-educational effort to "waken the arrested development in a group of autistic infants" (p. viii). There were "no special efforts" to teach the child "anything . . . of a specific nature" (p. 93). Instead, "the activities of the therapist" were "constantly and relentlessly directed at the child in such a way that the child could not escape the presence of the therapist" (p. 92). There was a persistent intrusion on the child's autistic preoccupations in ways that had

a highly stimulating quality to the . . . child, especially through a wide variety of tactile contacts, a great deal of motoric activities, and a constant effort at making sure that the child had demonstrated, through his behavior, that he had actually experienced the stimulation given (p. 92).

. . . the parents of each child in the project were recruited as the main psychotherapists and educators; and as many resources as were available in the community—teachers, pediatricians, ministers, etc.—were all made active coparticipants in the attempt we were making to awaken the child (p. viii).

The duration of the treatment program was 26 months for one child; 11 months for another child; and 14 months each for the three remaining children. Each child acted as his own control for this experiment: the child's status at the end of the project was compared with his initial status, by means of objective rating scales such as the Vineland, Fels, Cattell, Merrill-Palmer, Stanford-Binet, the Peabody, and the Leiter; as well as subjective observations by the clinical staff and reports from each child's parents and his teachers. All of the children made gains in social competencies, communicative skills, and level of functioning.

DesLauriers and Carlson suggest that once the autistic child's "affective barrier" is "transgressed" so that

> sensory messages can be received by him . . . his behavior in response will demonstrate an increasing capacity in him for appropriate affective reactions, for intelligent and adaptive behavior, for goal-directed and meaningful action, in the context of a normal family life (p. 91).

The five autistic infants in this study, they maintain,

> responded with such a degree of love for living that it is clear that what had appeared in them to be a strange form of death was really only a mysterious form of sleep. By awakening them to their own sense of humanity, we were able to open up for them the gates of learning; they showed us that they could grow and develop and learn, because there was a real purpose and value in doing so (p. 367).

However, this research project was abruptly terminated when renewed funding was denied, so the researchers could not fully test their hypothesis. "None of our children could be said to have reached completely such a degree of affective arousal that it could be considered self-sustaining" (p. 341), write the authors.*

A basic concomitant to the once-generally-held view that autism is psychogenic in origin was the premise that autistic children have no problems with language comprehension, and that the nonverbal autistic child is exhibiting "elective

---

* Reprinted with permission from DesLauriers and Carlson, *Your Child Is Asleep* (Homewood, Ill.: The Dorsey Press, 1969c.)

mutism"—that is, that he *can* speak, but refuses to do so. Logically, then, it followed that successful psychotherapy would not only resolve the child's intrapsychic conflicts, but also, in so doing, would simultaneously restore his speech. The consequence of this treatment approach was that most nonverbal autistic children remained mute into adulthood and beyond.

So speech training is a relatively new educational area for nonverbal autistic children. Lovaas has pioneered in developing techniques for establishing speech and other imitative behaviors in previously mute, inaccessible youngsters. His reports on his research (Lovaas, 1966a; 1966b; Lovaas *et al.*, 1966a; Lovaas *et al.*, 1966b; Lovaas, 1970) have received considerable critical review; some of it positive: among them, Jensen and Womack (1967), and Hingtgen, Coulter and Churchill (1967); and some of it highly negative: Bettelheim (1967) and DesLauriers and Carlson (1969), for example.

It must be remembered, however, that when Lovaas and his associates initiated their research, there were "no published, systematic studies on how to go about developing speech in a person who has never spoken" (Lovaas *et al.*, 1966a, p. 705). Because it has been observed that normal children develop speech by a process of imitation, Lovaas felt that the estabishment of imitative behavior in the mute, schizophrenic children with whom he worked was a logical starting point for building speech. "The first step in creating speech, then, was to establish conditions in which imitation of vocal sounds would be learned" (p. 705), say the authors.

A discrimination training procedure was developed, in which

Early in training, the child was rewarded only if he emitted a sound within a certain time after an adult had emitted a sound. Next he was rewarded only if the sound he emitted within the prescribed interval resembled the adult's sound. Toward the end of training, he was rewarded only if his vocalization very closely matched the adult's vocalization—that is, if it was, in effect, imitative. Thus verbal imitation was taught through the development of a series of increasingly fine discriminations (p. 705).*

Once the children had learned to imitate new words readily, the second part of the training program was introduced, in which the children were taught to associate meaning with words, and were taught the appropriate use of language.

Elsewhere in his writings, Lovaas (1966a; 1966b) describes the methodology which was used in teaching a child the correct names, or labels, of objects and behaviors in his environment; how to use, and respond to, prepositions, pronouns, and other abstractions, among them size, color, shape, et cetera; and finally, the use of conversational and spontaneous speech and language. Lovaas (1966a) concludes,

> One of the disadvantages of the program, as it now stands, lies in the large amount of time which is consumed in accomplishing its ends. It is fortunate, therefore, that the procedures can be easily communicated to parents and others who are emotionally committed to the child, and have the patience needed to carry them out. In fact, it seems highly likely that transfer and learning are of maximal benefit when the program is carried out in the child's ordinary day-to-day environment (p. 144).

In a speech delivered before the National Society for Autistic Children, Lovaas (1970) described methods for extinguishing self-destructive and other undesirable behaviors in autistic children; suppressing their bizarre, self-stimulatory mannerisms; and the expansion of their very limited behavioral repertoires, by teaching new behaviors.

Hewett (1965) outlines a year-long speech-training program he followed with a nonverbal four and one-half-year-old autistic boy, under which the child was first taught simple, hand imitation games; then the imitation of more complex tasks, like the assembly of simple puzzles; later the approximation of the

---

* Copyright 1966 by the American Association for the Advancement of Science. Reprinted with permission. Lovaas, O. I., Berberich, J. P., Perloff, B. F. and Schaeffer, B.: Acquisition of imitative speech by schizophrenic children. *Science, 151,* 3711 (Feb. 11): 705–707, 1966a.

teacher's vocalizations; and finally, the imitation of actual words.*

Still other writers and researchers, not previously mentioned here, have published reports of their experiments in developing effective educational approaches with autistic children: among them Ferster (1966); Clark (1965); Schopler and Reichler (1971); Rutter and Sussenwein (1971); Hingtgen, Sanders, and DeMyer (1965); Park (1967); *et cetera*. In a very interesting paper, Ney, Palvesky, and Markely (1971) report on the "Relative Effectiveness of Operant Conditioning and Play Therapy in Childhood Schizophrenia" (p. 337). Their approach revealed that operant conditioning is a more effective treatment tool than play therapy, in terms of the child's responsiveness and in the use of speech. The authors suggest further research to ascertain whether a combination of play therapy and operant conditioning might prove more effective than operant conditioning alone.

In discussing contemporary approaches to teaching autistic children, Wing and Wing (1966) write,

> One other approach, which may be called "regressive," rather than remedial, requires mention. In contrast to . . . other work . . . no systematic account and no scientific evaluation has been presented. The main features seem to be that the child is regarded as unwilling, rather than unable, to behave normally, that he understands speech perfectly and that many aspects of his behaviour indicate a desire to return to the breast . . . or to the womb. . . . A detailed description of the theory, the method and the results compared with those of remedial techniques is much needed (p. 202).

Bettelheim's *The Empty Fortress* (1967) purports to be that detailed accounting. Bettelheim claims to have had a "good outcome" (p. 414) with 42 percent of his autistic patients following years of intensive psychotherapy [as contrasted with

---

* Copyright, the American Orthopsychiatric Association, Inc., Reproduced by permission., Hewett, F. M.: Teaching speech to an autistic child through operant conditioning. *American Journal of Orthopsychiatry, 35*(5), 927–936, 1965.

a follow-up study by Eisenberg and Kanner (1956) in which they report a good adjustment in only 5 percent of their autistic patients. Eisenberg and Kanner conclude that psychotherapy is ineffective as a treatment method for autistic children].* In a 1968 review of *The Empty Fortress*, J. K. Wing writes

> The author's claim to have cured 17 out of 40 autistic children, and to have produced an improvement in 15 others, cannot be evaluated in the absence of information about selection, clinical symptomatology and disabilities, length of follow-up and the independence and reliability of diagnosis and assessments. Further data, collected according to the well-established criteria for conducting follow-up studies, will be awaited with interest. . . . Much better expositions are available elsewhere. . . . Those . . . who are willing to suspend a scientific attitude and read with the eye of faith, may find what they are looking for (p. 790).

This chapter makes no pretense of having included a comprehensive review of the available literature on the subject of successful teaching methods with nonverbal and verbal autistic children. What has been presented here is, however, a representative survey.

---

* Copyright, the American Orthopsychiatric Association, Inc., Reproduced by permission., Eisenberg, L. and Kanner, L.: Early infantile autism, 1943–1955. *American Journal of Orthopsychiatry, 26* (July): 556–566, 1956.

Chapter III

THE HANDICAPS OF AUTISTIC CHILDREN

THIS PAPER IS NOT particularly concerned with the causes of autism. However, because beliefs about causation can profoundly affect the educational approach that is followed with an autistic child, a brief discussion of the prevailing theories seems indicated.

There are two major schools of thought regarding the etiology:

The psychogenic hypothesis holds that autism is caused by environmental factors, primarily a personality disorder in the mother. But psychogenicists describe *both* father and mother as cold, detached "refrigerator-type" parents (Kanner, 1944, 1949,* Kanner and Eisenberg, 1955). Bettelheim is one of the foremost proponents of the psychogenic view: ". . . the precipitating factor in infantile autism is the parent's wish that his child should not exist" (1967, p. 125). The psychogenic hypothesis proposes psychotherapy as the only indicated treatment approach.

This theory of causation is refuted by: (a) studies in the literature, such as those by Spitz, dealing with children brought up in totally deprived institutional settings. None of these children became autistic. (b) Harlow's experiments with monkeys raised by "cruel, rejecting, unsympathetic and indifferent mothers" (Rimland, 1964, p. 44) demonstrated that the monkeys' reaction was a persistent attempt to gain the mother's attention, rather than an autistic withdrawal. (c) Most mothers of autistic children have normal children, as well (J. K. Wing,

---

* Copyright, the American Orthopsychiatric Association, Inc., Reproduced by permission., Kanner, L.: Problems of nosology and psychodynamics of early infantile autism. *American Journal of Orthopsychiatry, 19*(3), 416–426, 1949.

1966, pp. 33–34). Moreover, numerous researchers have attested to the ineffectiveness of psychotherapy as a treatment approach for autism (Rutter, 1966; Kanner and Lesser, 1958; Eisenberg and Kanner, 1956).

The second major hypothesis is the biological theory of causation. Arguments advanced in support of organic etiology include: (a) the fact that the condition occurs so early in life, and characteristically is accompanied by signs of brain damage, such as feeding difficulties and screaming; (b) the high male-female ratio (four boys to one girl); (c) the fact that in virtually every instance reported in the literature involving identical autistic twins, both twins were affected; and (d) the unique and specific nature of the symptoms (Rimland, 1964, pp. 51–52). According to J. K. Wing, ". . . the perceptual and speech difficulties . . . point to an abnormality in the central nervous system" (1966, p. 34). The biological hypothesis is supported by such researchers as Rutter (1966), Pribram (1970), Ritvo *et al.*, (1971), Taft and Cohen (1971), and others. There have also been a number of papers in the recent literature (Goodwin, Cowen, and Goodwin, 1971; Himwich *et al.*, 1972) suggesting that autism may be caused by a malfunction of the metabolism. Proponents of the biological hypothesis advocate remedial education: a teaching program for the autistic child in a highly structured environment, as the single most effective form of help presently available— *the* indicated treatment approach.

Sybil Elgar (1966) is among those who strongly support this view. As she puts it,

> . . . it is so often said that the fundamental deficiency in these children is that they have never been loved, that love is what they need to restore them to normality and that, once restored, they can subsequently learn in the same way as normal children. This is not an educational but a therapeutic approach—teaching is unnecessary, indeed contra-indicated, until the basic deficiency has been put right. I cannot too strongly emphasize my profound disagreement with this theory. . . . My pupils have parents who are an ordinary cross-section of humanity. Nearly all of them have other chlidren who are quite normal. They make mistakes in the same way as the parents of any type of

handicapped child but no more so. One wonders just how this view that the parents are cold and depriving originated. Perhaps if those who propagate it could have the experience of looking after an autistic child from birth, in their own families, we should hear less of the matter (pp. 205–206).

Despite the etiological theories that have been advanced, the bitter truth is that at this writing, there is no known cause and no known cure. Regardless of which of the two major hypotheses one supports, the fact remains that autistic children are cruelly deficient in their functioning. The basic premise underlying this chapter, then, is that autistic children are severely handicapped.

Prior to a meaningful discussion of teaching methods for autistic children, it is first necessary to describe the disabilities that they exhibit. Delineation of their specific cluster of deficiencies will explain why autistic children require specialized educational approaches; and concomitantly, will clarify the kinds of problems these specialized techniques are intended to ameliorate.

The basic objectives of education for autistic children are the same as those for all children: Hopefully, they will grow up "able to understand and enjoy the world" (Elgar, 1966, p. 205); skilled enough to be productively employed (in at least a sheltered situation); and sufficiently mature to behave and function in socially acceptable ways. So, as Elgar (1966) points out,

> The unique factors in the education of autistic children lie . . . not so much in the aims as in the methods whereby we hope to achieve the aims. . . . to understand what special methods are necessary, it is imperative to grasp the fact that the children are handicapped. Without the concept of handicap one has only the . . . reaction of pity, tenderness and tolerance, which will help the parents to help their children to develop as far as they are spontaneously able, but which will never help them overcome their specific disabilities, any more than love alone can teach a blind child to read Braille (p. 205).

What is an autistic child like, prior to educational treatment? Typically, they are attractive, graceful, and "strikingly intelligent" in appearance (Kanner, 1943, p. 247). Particularly in the young autistic child, social withdrawal is perhaps the most pronounced characteristic. Autistic children appear to be oblivious of other people, even their own parents and siblings. It is impossible to attract the child's attention by calling his name, or by speaking to him. It's as though he is ". . . living in a private, inaccessible dream-world; isolated, seemingly by choice, from contact with others" (Rimland, 1964, p. 5). Another peculiarity of these children is their seeming avoidance of direct eye contact. Typically the autistic child looks *through* people, rather than at them. There is not so much as the flicker of an eyelash to indicate his awareness of the presence of another person.

The children exhibit major disorders of speech and language. When speech is present, it is not communicative: the child makes parrot-like, nonconversational utterances. He isn't talking to anyone, or expecting an answer. Neither does he answer questions addressed to him; although some autistic children *do* answer questions by echoing the question. Thus if the child is asked, "Do you want some milk, dear?", he replies—in an exact imitation of the intonation and inflection of the questioner, "Do you want some milk, dear?" This phenomenon is referred to in the literature as "affirmation by repetition" (Rimland, 1964, quoting Kanner, p. 14). There may be considerable naming of objects; and echolalia, both immediate and delayed, is common. But the child never engages in conversation with others, nor does he initiate questions. When he does talk, his speech is marked by pronominal reversals: he refers to himself as "you," and to other people as "I." "You want a drink," one small autistic child used to tell his mother when he was thirsty. In general, the speech of verbal autistic children is characterized by its unusual voice quality: it is atonal and arythmic, and inflection is either absent or inappropriate.

About half of all autistic children remain nonverbal. Though they are not mute, since they do make sounds, speech is totally absent.

Still other characteristics of the autistic child include

the lack of imitative behavior, and his repetitive play activities and bizarre mannerisms. The child's total play repertoire may consist of flicking a piece of string; or spinning a jar lid; or rolling a ball. He will engage in a single activity of this kind for hours on end, and so intently that it is seemingly impossible to divert him. As Rimland puts it, "The child is often described as being . . . 'so completely wrapped up in his thoughts you can't talk to him' " (1964, p. 10). The strange mannerisms that the children exhibit include odd finger movements at the periphery of their eyes; peculiar arm flappings; unusual foot movements; and so on.

Autistic children are very difficult to live with. Tantrums are frequent; disturbed sleeping patterns are the rule rather than the exception; commonly, there are ritualistic eating and bedtime habits, and obsessive food preferences, as well as other peculiarities. Fortunately, once the child is placed in a school which offers an educational program that is geared to his needs, these behavioral anomalies begin gradually to recede and lessen in severity.

The underlying accompaniment of these maladaptive behaviors is a broad spectrum of disabilities. Autistic children have been described as "blind while seeing, and deaf while hearing" (Rimland, 1964, quoting van Krevelen, p. 99), because in their early years they are unable to make meaningful sense out of what they see and hear.

Numerous researchers have delineated what they conceive to be the children's deficiencies. To quote just a sampling:

> The autistic child is handicapped by a basic inability to integrate visual and auditory experiences into the meaningful patterns which form a basis for the normal child's developing understanding of the world (p. xi). . . . their basic disability may be analogous to that of the deaf-blind child in that they are unable, at first, to make meaningful patterns out of sensory stimuli, whether auditory or visual. The resulting behavioural abnormalities, together with the speech disorder, seem to be the most fundamental symptoms, while the various forms of odd behaviour and affective disturbance seem more likely to be related to an attempt by the child to meet the demands of the world with inadequate equipment for communicating (p. 6), (J. K. Wing, 1966, pp. xi–6).

The children have great difficulty in comprehending and using words and also in comprehending and using all but the simplest gestures and other forms of non-verbal communication (Collection of Papers, 1967, p. 51).

If one wished to make a 'recipe' for an autistic child, one would mix together the speech problems of receptive and expressive aphasic children, and the visual problems, the preference for using touch, taste and smell, and the odd bodily movements of children who have visual perceptual disorders. . . . In short, . . . autistic children suffer from multiple handicaps giving rise to disorders of perception, with subsequent problems of learning verbal and social skills. Their behavioural problems are more severe than children with only one or two handicaps. Adding another handicap more than doubles the secondary behavioural difficulties—each new perceptual problem reduces the possibility of compensating for the difficulties in understanding the world. An autistic child is blocked in almost all areas except for touch, taste, smell and movement. It is small wonder that he finds the world a bewildering place and his parents find him a bewildering person. Fortunately his handicaps do tend to improve as he grows older and he begins to be able to make some pattern out of the previous chaos (Lorna Wing, 1967, p. 13).

Clinical, comparative, and experimental studies of autistic children at all levels of intelligence have demonstrated the presence of a severe and extensive defect in language comprehension and in central functions associated with language and with the processing of symbolic or sequenced information. Circumstantial evidence suggests (but does not prove) that the language and cognitive defect constitutes the primary handicap in autism, the social and behavioral abnormalities arising as secondary consequences. . . . the consistent finding of gross language and cognitive deficits associated with autism and the consistent failure to find deviant factors in the environmental situation suggest that the language/cognitive impairment is the *main* factor involved in the pathogenesis of autism (Rutter and Bartak, 1971, p. 29).

In a compelling paper entitled *Multiple Impairments in Early Childhood Autism*, Wing and Wing (1971) compare the language, perceptual, motor, and behavioral abnormalities of autistic, receptive and expressive aphasic, partially blind and deaf, Down's syndrome, and normal children. They write,

The language problems are very prominent in autistic children, but there are other abnormalities as well. From the results of the comparative study described . . ., the following abnormalities can be listed: (a) visual perception problems, including a tendency to use peripheral rather than central vision, which although presumably of central origin are analogous to those found in children born both partially blind and partially deaf, with consequently similar preferences for exploring objects by means of touch, taste, and smell, and engaging in stereotyped movements; (b) difficulties in copying skilled movements, and in right-left and other directional orientation . . .; and (c) a paradoxical combination of hyper- and hyposensitivity of auditory, visual, and tactile input. In addition, immaturities of various aspects of physical development . . ., problems of postural control . . ., and abnormalities of autonomic function . . . have been described . . . (p. 261).

In an earlier paper, Wing and Wing (1966) subdivide the handicaps of autistic children into primary and secondary disabilities. In their view, the speech disorders and perceptual deficiencies are primary, whereas the strange behaviors and maladaptive social functioning are secondary characteristics, resulting from the child's efforts to cope with the demands of his environment in the light of his major communicative problems.

A recently-published paper by Churchill (1972) argues that the central language deficits which characterize autistic children are related to, but more severe than, those found in children with developmental aphasia. Churchill speaks of a "defect of language integration. . . . Such children, it seems, can be taught language 'performance' but not language 'competence'" (p. 185).

Churchill maintains that autistic children share with aphasic children

deficits which may cut across sensory modalities and which differ between individuals but are stable within individuals. . . . The two groups also share . . . sequencing problems and special problems with the meaning of words. Perhaps most devastating in terms of general language competence is the inability to handle the syntax or structure of language so as to be able to relate the word elements of a sentence independently to each other. . . . it is this which gives language its power and permits an individual not just to learn separately a limited number of word combinations but to understand and generate an infinite variety of sentences (p. 193).

In the next chapter, we will examine the specialized remedial education techniques which we have developed in the attempt to ameliorate, or compensate for, this formidable cluster of handicaps.

Before we proceed, however, it's important to understand that *all* of these disabilities are not necessarily found in every autistic child; and moreover, that the degree of handicap in specific areas will vary from child to child. For this reason, it is essential that there be an individual detailed evaluation and assessment of each child's strengths and weaknesses, as well as the level of his social maturity. Each child's program of remedial education should be geared to his specific spectrum of deficiencies and capacities. Actually, this applies to *all* handicapped children, not solely to autistics. But because autistic children are extremely difficult to test, there should be a close working relationship between teacher and consultant psychologist. Very often, the teacher, working with a child on a daily on-going basis, is able to elicit a level of performance from the child that the psychologist does not evoke within the confines of the psychological, test situation. Moreover, autistic children should be retested at relatively frequent intervals, with resultant alterations in the child's educational program as indicated by the child's test performance and the supplemental information the child's teacher is able to report to the psychologist, as well as the psychologist's direct observations of the child's classroom functioning. This affords an objective means of checking on a child's continuing progress. In this connection, Mittler (1966) writes,

> Assessment is now seen as essentially a continuous, dynamic process. It is coming to be appreciated that repeated testing is essential when dealing with handicapped children, and that a single assessment may be highly misleading. Furthermore, a variety of tests may need to be given, and for this purpose it is often necessary to see the child for more than one session.

Repeated testing is also necessary to obtain an estimate of *rate of development* over a period and to check on earlier indications of areas of specific difficulty. If the purpose of preliminary testing is to obtain a base line estimate, the fact that a formal test result, expressed in terms of IQ, cannot be obtained because the child is too disturbed or too uncooperative, it is not necessarily a reason for regarding him as untestable. It is important to record his behavior and any scorable result on all items that he does attempt, so that these can be used as a basis for comparison when he comes to be retested.

. . . The main purpose of psychological testing is to indicate areas of handicap so that advice on management and education can be given. . . . It follows from this that the closest cooperation between teacher and psychologist is indispensable. The psychologist has much to learn from the teacher about the validity of his test findings. It has often been observed that autistic children behave differently in the psychologist's office and in the classroom, and it is important to check on the validity of his test findings by observing the child in a teaching situation. He should also be in a position to assess the effect of his suggestions on the child in the classroom, and to modify the programme in consultation with the teacher. (pp. 147–149).

In our discussion of methods and techniques in the next chapter, then, it should be understood that the curriculum must be individually tailored for each child, and designed to ameliorate, or compensate for, his specific functional and developmental deficiencies.

Chapter IV

TEACHING TECHNIQUES

IN 1959, WHEN I began my first attempts to teach our non-verbal autistic son, Ethan, I knew that I was undertaking a formidable, and perhaps insuperable, task.

Ethan (then four and one-half years old) did not *look*, when I tried to show him how to do something; he gave no indication that he was *listening* to what I was telling him; and he made not the slightest effort to *imitate* the procedures I was trying to teach him.

How can one teach a child who doesn't look and doesn't listen and doesn't *do*?

I was not at that time a professional teacher, but I realized, simply on a common-sense basis, that there was one fundamental prerequisite which had to be accomplished before teaching of any kind could begin: Fortified by Dr. Kephart's assurance (Oppenheim, 1961) that I would not irreparably damage Ethan's psyche by making demands on him (advice which was, incidentally, diametrically opposite to everything we had been told by every clinician we had consulted prior to Dr. Kephart), I determined that the basic first step was to establish control, which meant, concomitantly, that I had to require Ethan to *attend*.

The ensuing battle of wills between Ethan and myself was a shattering experience for me—largely because this was, at that time, a revolutionary approach that contradicted every then-prevailing theory about appropriate treatment methods. But the resultant change in Ethan—because now he was at least accessible—taught me a lesson I have never forgotten: the establishment of control is *the* crucial first step in any educational program for autistic children, whether nonverbal or verbal.

How is this accomplished?

To begin with, by containing the child in the teaching

situation. It's advisable to start with an activity that the child can perform while sitting, simply because it's easier to contain a seated child than one who's trying to run from place to place around the room.

The second step in establishing control is to follow through on any command given to the child. This is imperative: the child *must* be required to perform. Supposing he can't, or won't? Then one takes the child's hands, and literally uses his hands to put him through the activity. It's important, then, to select tasks at the beginning that lend themselves to this kind of procedure.

With a very young child—say three, or even four, years of age, it's best to limit the duration of the required task at the outset to no more than five or ten minutes; and then give the child an equal amount of free time before bringing him back to the teaching situation for another activity. Gradually, the duration of each task is lengthened and the amount of free time between tasks is reduced, so that eventually the child's working periods correspond to those required of his classmates.

At the outset of a teaching program with an autistic child (and for a long time thereafter), he must be worked with on a one-to-one basis. So it makes little difference whether the setting is a school classroom where other children are present, or a clinical situation involving just the one child: the teacher *must* establish control from the very beginning of his work sessions with the child. Moreover, for a considerable period of time, it will be necessary to *re*-establish that control at the beginning of each subsequent lesson: Autistic children are generally extremely resistant to new learning situations, especially in the initial stages of their training. While this undoubtedly stems from the repeated failures the child has experienced in trying to cope with what seems to him to be a chaotic, incomprehensible world, it nevertheless creates an obstacle that the teacher must repeatedly meet and overcome.

A somewhat related, though not identical, difficulty which must be surmounted is the autistic child's tendency to "specialize" his output. For example: Once a teacher has succeeded in establishing (and re-establishing) control, the child will usually perform for *that* teacher on command; but the identical task presented by another teacher very often evokes the same resistance and refusal to perform that the first teacher experienced at the outset. Mittler's comment (1966) which we quoted in the last chapter, to the effect that autistic children are usually much less responsive in the psychologist's office than they are in the classroom, is a case in point. Wilson (1967) makes a similar observation:

> . . . there is always an interesting stage when they will look at their own teacher and nobody else. I go into a class quite often and I say "Hello, George" and George looks out of the window; but if the teacher says "George," George looks at the teacher (p. 36).

The solution to this problem is to accustom the child to work with a variety of teachers from the very outset—*each* of whom must establish control. In time, as he becomes used to working readily with several people, rather than with a single teacher, the child tends to become much less of a "specialist" in terms of whom he will perform for.

The teaching approach is very persistent: the teacher *intrudes*, very literally, on the child's detachment and avoidance of a given task; and the intrusion is implacable and unrelenting. Simultaneously, it must be conveyed to the child that the *teacher* is in control of the situation. The teacher communicates this by an attitude of quiet, calm certainty and confident expectancy. This is vital: autistic children cannot do their own structuring; they need to know that the adults in their environment are controlling their environment for them. In his own way, my son Ethan has confirmed this many times: for years, the criterion by which he judged a teacher's effectiveness was, "He's a good teacher, because he knows how to boss me."

When an autistic child initially enters a school situation, very often his disturbed behavior is the most immediate problem to be met. It's essential that the child never be permitted to escape a task because of a tantrum, or because of violent or self-destructive behavior. Neither should the child's physical resistance to the task, such as wriggling his hands while the teacher is trying to put him through, say, a buttoning procedure, for example, be a deterrent. It may be necessary to interrupt the task and isolate the child (with adult supervision) until the tantrum is over; but once he is calm again, he should immediately be brought back to the task which triggered the behavior. Similarly, the child who attempts to bite, pinch, kick or scratch his way out of a lesson may need to be restrained to discourage his aggression, but this must never be a successful means of task avoidance.

Furthermore, for quite some time, each attempt to teach the child a more complex skill than he has already learned, may lead to a recurrence of resistant behavior. As a concomitant of their difficulty in processing sensory information, autistic children tend to become comfortable all too readily with their learning-wise status quo. This is, in some ways, related to the symptom that Kanner (1943) described as their insistence on the preservation of sameness. So for a considerable period of time, each new learning situation is threatening to the child; and he will use every device in his repertoire of resistance to avoid the task. It is vital that these resistant behaviors prove to be consistently unsuccessful, in literally every single instance. Once the more-difficult task is presented to the child (and the teacher believes it to be within the child's capabilities), the teacher *must* require the child to perform it—modified somewhat, if need be—regardless of the magnitude of the child's resistance. It's imperative that the teacher win every one of these battles of will. Fortunately, as the child builds up a growing experiential background of successes, his self-confidence increases and his self-image improves; and there is a resultant gradual decline in the frequency and intensity of his negativism.

To interject a seemingly contradictory note at this point: We have thus far attributed the child's refusal to attempt new tasks entirely to resistance. However, this is not altogether justified. The autistic child is deficient, not only in the ability to imitate, but also in his ability to *initiate* new motor patterns. So the child's failure to perform does not always stem solely from negativism. At least some of the time, it is due to his major difficulty in initiating a new activity. Thus, while Rimland (1964) writes that ". . . refusal to use the hands is a fairly common symptom" (p. 12), we think that this is not always an *elective* refusal: we maintain that autistic children have an output problem, and are literally unable to consciously and volitionally activate their hands in certain instances when it is necessary for them to monitor their performance. Very often, at these times, the child's hands are so limp that it is almost as though there are no bones beneath the skin. In such a situation, putting the child through the task by manipulating his hands is a means of feeding in the required motor patterns kinesthetically. This is a way of teaching the child via three simultaneous sensory modalities: kinesthetically, by the motor manipulation of the child's hands; visually, since one *requires* him to look; and auditorially, with a brief accompanying oral description of what the child is doing. In time, the child becomes able to take on the task on his own. (It should perhaps be mentioned here, parenthetically, that a study undertaken by Lovaas *et al.*, (1971) involving the simultaneous presentation of auditory, visual, and tactile cues, suggests that autistic children are overselective in their attention to stimulus inputs, and attend to only *one* stimulus at a time: if they are listening, they tend to block accompanying visual stimuli, and when they are taking in information visually, they do not hear; etc. This would seem to imply that teaching an autistic child via more than one sensory modality simultaneously is futile. However, it is not yet known to what extent the findings of Lovaas and his associates apply to *all* autistic children; and there is also the possibility that continuing to teach in this way may develop the child's deficient abilities to attend to more than one stimulus in a complex stimulus situation. In the absence of more extensive evidence to the contrary, we will continue to advocate this method of teaching.)

This is one way of circumventing the autistic child's problems in processing visual and auditory information. For example, one autistic boy learned to ice skate as the result of his parents' manipulation of his legs and feet in the required gliding movement, across their livingroom rug. Showing him how to glide had been ineffective, because he had not yet developed sufficient imitative ability; and of course *telling* him how to glide would at that time have been beyond the limits of his comprehension. At the beginning, the teacher may have to use this kinesthetic method of teaching for a great many different kinds of activities, some of them involving not just the hands, but the feet, legs, and/or body, as well. Though we developed this teaching approach independently, this is obviously similar to that used by Elgar (1966). She writes, "Much of the teaching, at least initially, must be conducted by touch— the child's hands or feet or body being guided into appropriate postures or movements" (p. 208). In time, as the child progresses, his repertoire of independently-performed activities develops and grows in a variety of areas; and concurrent with this, there is a growing development of the ability to imitate, based solely on visual information. Eventually, the child becomes able to perform independently on command.

The teacher must develop an intuitive sensitivity, however, about when—or whether—to intervene, and motorically put the child through an activity. At the outset, most autistic children will require this. But the teacher must *always* first give the child an opportunity to perform independently. It is only when it becomes apparent that this is not going to occur that the teacher steps in and manipulates the child's limbs for him.

Conversely, the teacher must be equally perceptive about subsequently getting himself *out* of the activity. It's important that the child be encouraged to perform independently at the earliest possible moment. Sometimes this involves teacher insistence that the child take over the task. Autistic children tend to become dependent on any kind of a crutch very readily; and a perceptive teacher knows instinctively when the crutch is no longer necessary. With some children, an abrupt withdrawal of direct teacher manipulation of the child's limbs, is all that's needed. More frequently, the teacher fades his assistance from actually manipulating the child's hands, for example, to merely holding the child's hands while the youngster is actually performing the task himself, to then just touching the child's hands with one finger, and finally to no physical contact at all.

Still another basic precept: The teacher must not permit the child to engage in autistic mannerisms and/or bizarre behaviors during a work-session. To the extent that it is possible to eliminate these, it is important that they *be* eliminated. These children are capable of only a limited amount of directed output and if they dissipate it in these autistic mannerisms, this both diverts their attention and decreases the amount of energy they have available for the optimum performance of the task at hand. In general, however, the child is less apt to engage in abnormal and atypical behaviors when he is kept occupied, as much of this kind of behavior stems from boredom. So the task itself contributes, at least in part, to the elimination of the behavior. Unfortunately, however, the reverse is also true: if the child feels threatened by the task, as autistic children so frequently do, at least in the initial stages of their training, then it results in an *increase* in the bizarre mannerisms; and teacher intervention to prevent it becomes a *must* if the necessary learning is to occur.

We have referred several times in this chapter to the fact that the child must be required to *attend* during a lesson period. This means that he must *look* at the lesson materials; that he must *see* what his hands are doing when he is engaged in an activity; that he must *watch* what is happening to his hands, arms, feet, legs, head, and/or body when he is being "put through" a procedure (a mirror is sometimes helpful here); and that he must then *observe* the end result. He must be made to *listen* to an explanation or description of how something is to be done and so on. In short, the child's attention must be fixed on the teacher and on the on-going activity; nothing else. How is this accomplished? By physically taking his chin, for example, if his head is turned away, and turning his head in the appropriate direction so his eyes *can* focus on the activity. By drawing his eyes in to the task: if his gaze has wandered, it's possible to startle the child back to attending by a sudden clap of the teacher's hands, or by a slam of the teacher's hand on the desk, or by saying "*Look!*" either loudly or softly as the circumstances dictate. The teacher can pull the child's eyes in to the task by taking the child's index finger and tapping the lesson materials with it. In time, the child becomes better able to sustain a visual focus without help. It should be mentioned, parenthetically, that many autistic children seem to have better peripheral than foveal vision so that very often when it appears that the child is not looking, he may, in fact, be seeing precisely what the teacher wants him to look at. But there is no way that one can be sure that he has actually looked unless he can be observed to focus foveally on the proffered materials. Besides, the child should be encouraged to use his central vision. So it's important that the teacher work with the child from a position where he/she can constantly watch the child's eyes. Similarly, there is no way to *insure* the child's listening to what is being said to him. What the teacher *can* do, however, is to create optimum circumstances for listening: if the child is singing, or humming, or babbling, he should be told to stop; and if the verbal command to stop is ineffective (and it very often is, especially at the outset), then the teacher puts his finger across the child's lips, in the "Sh!" position, or even holds the child's lips gently together, if need be.

The common denominator of every activity in which one engages the child is that the child must be praised and rewarded for all acceptable behavior, whether it be teacher-directed or self-initiated. At the outset, every minute increment of acceptable behavior and every tiny bit of progress must be praised—and rewarded, if the program uses tangible rewards like candy or some other treat. In our school, for example, a child habitually resisted standing on his own two feet during the morning Pledge of Allegiance by letting his body go limp and dropping to the floor. He was lauded and given a candy M&M the first dozen or so times that he stood up straight and still during the Pledge. It's essential that even very small gains win approval and reinforcement so that the child repeatedly experiences success and its accompanying tangible and intangible satisfactions. It's equally important that approval be communicated to the child in ways he can't mistake—

by gestures of pleasure and affection and by means of enthusiastic verbal and facial expression. Even when an autistic child can't comprehend precisely what's being said to him he's very perceptive in his interpretation of intonation and inflection.

In general, as the child grows older, provided he has been attending a highly-structured school program with a curriculum geared to his particular needs, his handicaps lessen, and under the tutelage of teachers who understand and deal with his special spectrum of disabilities, he becomes increasingly manageable and teachable. By adolescence, many of the behavior problems we have described have for the most part subsided. This varies in degree, of course, from child to child, but usually with adolescents, a skilled teacher who understands autistic children is no longer so concerned with managing the child's behavior so that he *can* be taught. This part of the problem has been largely overcome. Now the teacher's efforts must be concentrated in such areas as developing methods of overcoming the youngster's lack of initiative, or of instilling greater confidence, and so on. Of course, adolescent autistics, like their younger counterparts, tend to have "good" days and "bad" days. It seems likely that their "bad" days, with the accompanying erratic behavior, stem from physiological factors of undetermined origin.

What we have outlined, so far in this Chapter, are the *general* methods we use in the teaching of autistic children, the "treatment" part of our educational-treatment approach. In this connection, Elgar (1966) argues that ". . . it is no part of the teacher's job to 'treat' children" (p. 211); and Wing and Wing (1966) point out, "Teaching is not an inferior form of psychotherapy, and should not be confused with 'treatment' at all . . ." (p. 196). We concur fully with both Elgar and the Wings; but we maintain that for autistic children, education *is* treatment. In her Foreword to *Autistic Children* (Lorna Wing, 1972), Despert writes, "Therapy, in the case of autism, must come from *outside*—education rather than interpretation of inner life" (p. vii). It's in that context, as synonymous with methodology, that we use the term "treatment" here.

Before we begin a description of techniques, let us first briefly consider setting and curriculum.

So that autistic children may live at home with their families, we advocate a day school setting, one which follows a developmental approach in an educational milieu. Sometimes, specific circumstances make it impossible for a family to keep their autistic child at home; when these exist, placement in a good residential school is the necessary alternative. But generally speaking, the optimum situation is for the child to live at home and attend a day school as his normal siblings do. We think autistic children need a highly structured program in which they are required to perform, a learning environment that is ". . . structured, organized and logical rather than 'permissive'" (Wing and Wing, 1966, p. 194).

Because autistic children need so much individual attention in order to learn, there must be a high teacher-child ratio—at least one full-time teacher and two full-time aides for a five-child class. There are people in the field who argue that there should be one staff person for each child. Autistic children, and particularly the nonverbal autistic child, will do so little without direct one-to-one teacher supervision, especially in the early stages of their school enrollment, that we can see the logic in this position. Nevertheless, we do not agree with it; we feel that if *everything* is structured for the child, if he is *never* given an opportunity to manipulate materials in the school setting without supervison, then we are creating a functional cripple—a child who may eventually perform well in a one-to-one situation with an adult, but who requires 100 percent attention from an adult in order to perform at all. We think a more optimum arrangement is one where each child receives about fifteen to twenty minutes of one-to-one teaching in each half hour time segment, and for the remaining ten to fifteen minutes the child is given a manual manipulative task or an academic-related activity of some kind, an assignment that's on a realistic level for that child in terms of his functioning, to perform independently without direct teacher supervision. The objective here is for the child to develop a repertoire of activities which he can do completely on his own. The weakness in this approach is that very often, especially in the early stages of his school enrollment, the child will totally ignore the work materials on his desk while he engages in his autistic rituals. Nevertheless, with an occasional verbal prod from the teacher while she is working with another youngster, it's possible to draw the child back to the task so that he'll do at least part of it. In time, with this approach, he may ultimately perform the entire task on his own. We think it's worth the gamble. Each small bit of independently completed work should call forth warm praise, affection, and in the beginning stages, a tangible reward.

The physical setting should include a room where a child who is having a tantrum can be isolated (with an attending adult) until he is quiet again. It is important, however, in most cases, that the tantrumous child not be rewarded with *too* much attention. A too-solicitous, hovering adult merely serves to reinforce the tantrum behavior. The message the child gets is, "The more I scream and carry on, the more attention I'll get"; and what such adult conduct communicates to the child's seemingly oblivious classmates is, "A *sure* way to get attention is to have a tantrum." It is much better to place the child in an isolation room from which all possible booby traps have been eliminated. In a setting where it's impossible for the child to harm himself, (a self-destructive child should be placed in a restraint of some kind) or damage the premises, he can safely be ignored in most instances. Usually the tantrum will be over in relatively short order.

The curriculum is not too unlike that in a school for normal children except that it must, of necessity, include the teaching of many self-care and socialization skills, and the building in of understandings and behaviors that the normal child learns almost automatically just in the process of daily living. In addition, the program should include speech and language training, listening activities and teaching in the traditional academic areas of reading, writing and mathematics. For those children who progress sufficiently, science, social studies, and the like should be included. Games and other activities designed to promote social behavior and peer interaction; manual manipulative activities which should in time lead into the training of work-orientation and prevocational skills, and ultimately vocational training; gross motor work and the teaching of body image concepts; and other activities, such as visual training, arts and crafts, and music are essential too. [1]

Teaching socialization involves training in a variety of self-care and social skill areas: personal cleanliness and grooming, buttoning, fastening together and zipping a zipper, tying shoelaces, table manners, setting the table properly, knowing how to cross a street safely, and so on. In the main, these skills are taught by the methods we described earlier: initially, the teacher feeds in the appropriate motor patterns by manually manipulating the child's hands and fingers, and in time, the child takes over the task on his own.

The importance of training socialization skills can not be overemphasized. The more self-managing the autistic child is, the greater the possibility of his leading a meaningful and productive life in adulthood. Research studies have shown that while there is no direct correlation between tested IQ and job success among the mentally handicapped population (Cowan and Goldman, 1967), there is a significant correlation between the level and degree of socialization skills and ultimate job success in either a sheltered work situation or on the open labor market (Baronyay, 1971; Tobias and Gorelick, 1967; Kolstoe, 1967). As yet, there have been no similar studies with autistics, *per se*, but certainly any advances that the autistic child makes in socialization skills are a positive improvement in his social maturity, regardless of his ultimate employability, and these should be taught on a regular, on-going basis.

So, to the extent that this is possible and feasible for a specific child, training in self-care skills, personal hygiene and grooming; social interaction with his peers; crossing a street without supervision—these should all be part of the daily curriculum. The older autistic child, depending on his level of functioning, should be taught how to use public transportation without supervision, the independent use of both public and home telephones and appropriate telephone manners, money value knowledge and the ability to make purchases independently. Boys should learn how to shave themselves. Still other necessary socialization skills involve recognition of, and appropriate response to signs and their meanings, i.e. Men's Room, Danger, and so on; recognition of situations which may be hazardous or in which help may be required, including methods of requesting assistance; training in leisure time activities; knowing how to open a can of food and heat its contents; making a sandwich; putting a frozen dinner into the oven, and removing it when it is edible, and so on.

Training in socialization is an important part of the daily curriculum, but it is *only* a part. It is *not* a substitute for the teaching of more traditional educational skills, which should also be an integral part of the daily curriculum.

Unlike some other educators and some of the researchers in the field, we are not concerned in our teaching approach with autistic children with establishing contact, *per se*, as a prerequisite to the beginning of more formal teaching. It has been our experience that in the process of teaching the child even very basic skills, the teacher can succeed in getting eye contact from the child, that the teaching process itself results in a mutual interaction between teacher and child and that the eventual outcome is the establishment of a developing and growing relationship between them. We disagree with Wilson's contention (1966) that "The autistic child has difficulty in learning because he does not pay attention" (p. 177). An effective teacher of autistic children knows how to gain and hold the child's attention. Elgar's concept (1966) of the basic educational problem, on the other hand, mirrors our own view: "Withdrawal, avoidance of eye-to-eye contact, and the rest are *not* the most important or the most significant aspects of the condition. The speech and visual learning difficulties are" (p. 211).

Speech is certainly a major problem; a formal period of daily speech training on a one-to-one basis with a speech therapist is a *must* for every child in the program. The methods outlined by Lovaas (1966a and b), as briefly described in Chapter 2 of this paper, are, we think, the most effective thus far developed for teaching speech to mute autistic children. Developing communicative speech in echolalic youngsters is also a difficult teaching task, but Lovaas, as well as a number of other researchers, among them Risley and Wolf (1967) and Sapon (1972), have developed successful techniques for overcoming this problem. However, in the initial stages, the direct teaching of speech to nonverbal children should not be a classroom procedure because it is such a time-consuming process.

In this connection, a distinction must be made between the nonverbal child and the *essentially* nonverbal (or echolalic) child. Neither is able at the outset of his school attendance to use speech for communication. However, despite the fact that some clinicians tend to categorize both types of autistic children as nonverbal, there is, in fact, a major difference between them. The echolalic child is noncommunicative but he is *not* nonverbal. He has speech even though he lacks oral language. This means that he begins his school attendance with at least a foundation of reasonably well-articulated speech. He is *already* able to imitate speech; and the further development into communicative speech can be accomplished by skillful shaping in an encouraging, speech-oriented classroom program supplemented by daily individual speech therapy.

The autistic child who is still nonverbal at the time of his school enrollment, however, lacks even imitative speech—which means that he has not yet developed even the ability to volitionally control his speech mechanism and oral musculature for the production of speech. For this youngster, particularly if he's seven or eight years old or older, encouragement alone will *not* result in imitative speech. Such a child will *not* develop speech spontaneously. Nevertheless, with the use of Lovaas-type methods in a one-to-one speech therapy situation, even the older nonverbal autistic child can usually be helped to develop speech. How *much* speech an older child will acquire and how well articulated it will be is impossible to predict. With some nonverbal youngsters, the development of speech seems to be facilitated by a global approach that adds the teaching of manual communication (sign language) to formal speech training *per se* and the ongoing teaching of phonics and spelling skills in the reading program. Teacher and speech therapist should work very closely together; once the child has acquired even very rudimentary speech, his lessons in the classroom should be designed so that the child can be required to use his speech in appropriate situations.

From the very beginning of each child's school enrollment, language training is a vitally important classroom activity. To a greater or lesser degree, every autistic child has problems with language comprehension. We use a variety of procedures to facilitate increasing comprehension: associating the name of an object with the object; matching pictures and objects; selecting the designated noun picture from among a multiple choice grouping, when the teacher says, "Show me the picture of the bird," and so on. There is a logical progression to the process from simple to increasingly complex. Thus, in time, the child is asked to generalize: Can he match pictures of similar, but not identical, objects, such as a ruler and a tape measure? Can he associate an object with its function? For example, if he is told, "Give me the picture of the thing that you would wear on your head," can he select the picture of the hat from among a multiple choice grouping placed before him? Still another way of building comprehension involves dramatizing verbs; for example, the teacher takes Johnny's hand in hers, and together they run down the corridor, while the teacher chants, "Run, Johnny, run. Johnny is running. Teacher is running. We are running." In a similar fashion, the child can be taught to develop a motor awareness of such concepts as over, under, in, on top of, et cetera. The curriculum also includes concepts of size, height, depth, position, direction, and tactile discriminations, such as smooth-rough, soft-hard; even concepts of tempo are included, such as "Walk fast; walk slowly," and so on.

A few words here about methodology: It's important that commands and instructions that are given to the child be brief. The teacher talks in short, simple sentences at least during the early stages of training. Another important consideration is that the task be structured in such a way that a correct response is possible. For example, the nonverbal child can't give an oral response. Neither do most autistic children below the age of about eight (and sometimes well past that age) have a definitive one-finger point. So, in presenting materials to the child, say a grouping of pictures or objects in a situation where the child has to indicate the one that the teacher has orally designated, it's essential that these be spaced far enough apart on the child's desk that, even if he uses his whole hand to point with, there is still no doubt about which one the child is selecting.

Still another basic: drill—requiring the child to repeat the same task in the same way day after day in an effort to help him acquire a particular concept which he seems to find it difficult to learn—should be avoided. Drill is as unproductive with the autistic child as it is with the normal child. Moreover, because of the autistic child's rigidity and addiction to sameness, drill is contraindicated. Redundancy: teaching the same concept in a variety of different ways and, where feasible, via various sensory modalities is a much more effective teaching approach. For example, to teach a child the concept of under, the teacher may illustrate the concept by placing a block under a cup, and telling the child, "The block is *under* the cup." The child can then be given two objects and told, "Put the book *under* the bowl." If he doesn't understand what's required, he can be put through the procedure. The teacher may tell the child, "Find the wastebasket *under* the desk." The child may be required to crawl *under* the table, to place something on the shelf which is *under* the counter, and so on. Each of the required tasks is different, yet each conveys the concept of under.

Particularly for the mute autistic child, but also for the echolalic youngster (because it is usually very difficult to evoke an appropriate oral response from a child who has speech, but has only minimal language), it's vital that the materials be adapted so the child can demonstrate what *he* knows. Telling is not teaching! To illustrate: One of the activities we use with our prereading children is the interpretation of picture stories. For these, we prepare multiple choice answers to a series of detailed questions about the stories. Each of these answers is printed on a separate card. We put the question to the child, and set the answer cards before him. "Billy, show me Spot. Good! Why is Spot barking?" Now we read each card aloud to him, making sure that Billy knows which card says what. An absolutely crucial prerequisite for this task, as for any other, is that the teacher must be *sure* that the child actually looks at the material presented to him, and moreover, that he looks at each part of the material. One of the ways to do this is for the teacher to sit directly across the desk from Billy where she can observe his eyes as she takes his index finger in her hand and says, "Look, Billy," and then taps his finger firmly on each of the answer cards in turn as she reads it aloud to him. We have found that the combination of the auditory command to look together with the tactual stimulus the child gets from the tapping of his own finger seems to facilitate directing his visual attention to the desired stimulus. In this instance, tap, "Because he sees another dog on TV." Tap, "Because he wants to go out." Tap, "Because he's hungry." Billy is then required to indicate the correct answer.

Listening activities are also an important part of the curriculum. Autistic children can hear, but because in their early years most of what they heard was a meaningless jumble, they have become very adept at tuning out what they hear by the time they enter school. However, listening is a learned skill so it can be taught. During every lesson period, whenever it is appropriate, the teacher is verbalizing *for* the child and simultaneously encouraging *him* to verbalize. The objective is to develop and awaken the child's dormant listening skills. The teacher names the object (or letter, or word) that the child is matching or reads aloud the answer that the child has selected. (Timing is a major factor, here; the teacher shouldn't "jump the gun" before the child has made his choice or has otherwise had the opportunity to show his knowledgability or lack of it in the given work area.) In addition, we use a multitude of procedures to develop listening skills. Among them, we play a game with a buzzer board which involves the child's selecting, from among a multiple choice grouping, the card that has the same pattern imprinted on it as the teacher played on the buzzer board, i.e. short-long-short-long. Another game requires the child to choose, from a series of pictures (or objects) set before him, the picture whose name rhymes with the word that the teacher says. For still another game, the child must listen as we strike the table top with a mallet and then indicate the numeral that tells how many times the mallet hit the table. Other listening activities involve the child's identifying the picture (such as a train, a dog, et cetera) of whatever is making the environmental sound being played on a tape recorder or the picture that depicts a particular incident in a story being told on the tape. At a somewhat more difficult level, the child listens to a series of words, and then selects the picture that starts with the same sound as the spoken words, and so on. Actually, most of the activities in which the children engage in the classroom require listening as a prerequisite for performance.

A word of caution here about the use of multiple choice groupings: The teacher must be careful to vary the placement of the correct answer constantly, using a random pattern of placement. Only by this means can we be sure that the child is in fact making the correct choice, rather than selecting an answer solely on the basis of its position.

In the more traditional educational areas, academic work, we also follow the customary progression from the simple to the more complex. The only difference between our approach and that in the ordinary elementary school classroom is that we adapt our methods, our materials, and our techniques to the individual disabilities of our children. To teach reading, for example, we begin at the readiness level. We start with color matching and color identification, then proceed to the matching of geometrical forms and the identifying of each form by name. Once we have established that the child can make gross discriminations between various geometrical forms and associate the name of the form with its shape, we introduce other concepts. Can the child differentiate between large and small, big and little, tall and short? Can he reply appropriately to the question, "Which one is different?" about a series of seemingly identical pictures, only one of which differs from the others in color, size, direction or in more subtle ways—perhaps because a relatively inconspicuous part is missing? Is he able to arrange pictures in sequence so that they tell a story? Can he make fine enough visual discriminations to match letters of the alphabet and pairs of words? Is his auditory discrimination sufficiently acute that he can discern the initial sound of a word and associate it with the consonant letter that has the same sound? Wherever applicable, we use simultaneous sensory modalities—auditory, visual, tactile and kinesthetic—to reinforce the child's learnings. Eventually the child is ready to match words to objects and/or pictures and pictures and objects to words.

The next step involves choosing the appropriate word from among a multiple choice grouping (*sans* pictures) set before him in order to correctly supply the missing word in a sentence the teacher has dictated to him. For example, for the sentence, "I will have an _____ for breakfast," the child would supply the word, egg. At a slightly more advanced level, the child is given a card on which there is a short sentence with one word left blank. The child must read the sentence and then select the appropriate completing word from among several choices set before him, each printed on a separate card. For example, for the sentence "I drink _____," the missing word could be "milk"; for "I eat _____," the correct word could be "cookies"; for "I wear a _____," the completing word could be "shirt," and so on. We make it a point to use only grammatically-correct sentence structure in exercises of this nature. We do not approve of presenting the child with the kind of "pidgin English" that some workers in the field employ with autistic children.

Our teaching is geared toward the practical, daily-life application of early reading skills, and comprehension is built in from the very outset. Thus, another reading activity is a "Read and Do" lesson: using a magnetic fishpole, the child makes a "catch"—a slip of paper (with a metal clip) on which we have written a simple command, "Clap your hands," or "Close the door," or "Bounce the ball." The child is required to read the instruction, and then *do* it.

An important part of all of our reading lessons involves encouraging the child to verbalize the reading material, to the extent of his capability. This is done during each step of the lesson, but only *after* the child has indicated the correct answer. The timing is important here, for these reasons: First, we want to be sure that the child is actually *reading* the material, rather than responding to a subtle clue that the teacher may be unwittingly giving in urging the child to talk. Our second reason is that once the child has chosen his answer, the teacher can freely provide him with a prompt to stimulate speech if need be, or correct the child's articulation if this is indicated, without being concerned about inadvertently revealing the answer to the reading material.

Still another reading procedure is particularly useful with those children whose reading proficiency is greater than their ability to control the pencil for writing. The child is asked to "compose" a story, in this fashion: The teacher asks the child a question, and the child is then required to read and select the words that form a sentence in reply. For instance, the first question might be, "What is your name?". The teacher then presents the child with five small cards, on each of which a pronoun is printed, say: You, I, Your, His. When the child makes his choice, he pastes the card on a sheet of paper. Now the teacher gives the child a second group of five cards, perhaps mane, nome, nema, mean, name. The word the youngster selects is fastened next to the first word on the sheet of paper. And so on, until the sentence is completed. The teacher has been saying each word aloud after each selection. With a nonverbal child, the teacher now reads the entire sentence orally as the child points to each word in turn. Then the teacher asks a second question—perhaps, "How old are you?". Only two questions are used at the outset. Later, these stories can be expanded to three, four, or even more sentences, in accordance with the increasing development of the child's reading abilities. Our children usually enjoy this activity, and show pleasure in hearing their stories. As a rule, they have no difficulty in composing grammatical sentences. Admittedly, the choices we give them are errorless in that they are limited to the correct parts of speech—i.e., only nouns where a noun is required, only verbs where a verb is needed, and so on. But in each instance, the child must select the *correct* pronoun or noun or whatever. This leads us to question Churchill's assertion (quoted in Chapter III) that autistic children lack the ability "to handle syntax or structure of language so as to be able to relate the word elements of a sentence . . . to each other" (1972, p. 193).

Our reading program also incorporates the use of basal and/or programmed readers, adapting them as each child's verbal deficiencies dictate. As the children's reading abilities grow, we progress gradually to higher reading levels. Most of the autistic children whom we have taught have learned to read without difficulty, often before they develop speech.

Writing, however, is another story. Many autistic youngsters have major problems in controlling pencils, chalk, or crayons. This disability appears to be more pronounced in nonverbal children, but there are, of course, variations of degree from child to child. Depending on the child and his specific deficiencies in this area, we usually teach writing (following earlier instruction in drawing lines, circles, crosses, and other geometrical forms) by manipulating the child's hand, and thus feeding in the motor patterns. We believe that the autistic child's difficulties with writing stem from a definite apraxia just as the nonverbal child's troubles with articulation do when speech finally develops. There seems to be a basic deficiency in certain areas of his motor expressive behavior. So, in teaching writing, we find that it is usually necessary to continue to guide the child's hand for a considerable period of time. Gradually, however, we are able to fade this to the mere touch of a finger on the child's writing hand. We're uncertain about precisely what purpose this finger-touching serves. What we *do* know is that the quality of the writing deteriorates appreciably without it despite the fact that the finger is in no way guiding the child's writing hand. "I can't remember how to write the letters without your finger touching my skin," one nonverbal child responded when he was asked why he would not write unless he was touched. Certainly the children do evince problems in executing the forms of the various letters and numbers. The problem is not recognition, but rather execution, in retaining the mental image of required motor patterns. Ultimately, however, the finger-touching can be eliminated, and the child does write without it, although some children want the touch of a finger on some other bodily surface, such as the head, in order to write. One of our children who had progressed to writing on his own had great difficulty in remembering how to write numerals despite his good abilities in arithmetic. He solved his problem by copying the appropriate numeral from the classroom clock.

We teach cursive rather than manuscript writing from the beginning because the continuous pencil strokes required to complete a word in cursive writing are more conducive to uninterrupted performance.

As a rule, autistic children learn mathematics very readily. Many of these youngsters seem to have an affinity for math and some of them demonstrate phenomenal abilities in this area. We use the traditional procedures adapted to the needs of the individual child and presented in a way that enables a nonverbal child, or one with minimal speech, to show unequivocally how much he knows and understands. The children are required to manipulate concrete materials for the development of sound basic numbers concepts. It's not uncommon for a child to demonstrate a grasp of abstract concepts at a much higher level than his manipulation of the concrete mathematical materials would indicate.

Circle games and similar activities, such as playing catch, relay races, and the like, are intended to promote social exchanges among the children. Usually, however, the children interact with the adults in their environment much more readily than they do with their peers, and since as a rule they have no interest in winning, *per se*, they almost never display the competitive spirit that relay races require. Nevertheless, these are part of the normal childhood experience; and circle games, such as "Did you ever see a laddie" serve the additional purpose of helping the child to consciously initiate motor behaviors when it is his turn to be the leader. They contribute to the development of imitative behavior as well. Another benefit is the reinforcement of body image concepts. At the outset, we usually have to put the child through the motions of the various games, but in time he develops the ability to copy movements and skill in catching, throwing, and bouncing a ball, and so forth.

We use a variety of manual manipulative materials in our program: lacing cards; jigsaw puzzles; pegboards; people puzzles consisting of pieces of the same size and shape so that the child *must* attend to the content rather than the shape of the pieces in order to complete the task; form boards; beads and string; bead patterns; block patterns; three-dimensional patterns; relatively intricate tactile parquetry patterns; *et cetera*. Initially, the child is taught how to work with these materials in one-to-one sessions with a teacher. Subsequently, it is these same materials which we present to the child to work with, independently with no supervision, between his turns for individual tutoring. We have a two-fold objective here: we want to expand the child's repertoire of activities that he will do on his own without requiring one-to-one teacher attention; and we want to develop the child's manual and eye-hand coordination skills which are concomitantly work-orientation skills so that he will acquire increasing facility in areas that may have some ultimate vocational utility.

Gross motor work and training in body image concepts is an integral part of our program. Generally, we alternate periods of seated activity with periods of motor activity so that we can provide the children with an acceptable tensional outlet at relatively frequent intervals. Though autistic children usually appear to be very graceful in their volitional use of their bodies, they tend to have difficulty in acquiring motor skills in situations where they are required to monitor their movements consciously. The thrust of our gross motor training is the development of body image concepts; helping the child to achieve laterality, which involves an inner sense of rightness and leftness; directionality, which is the projection of laterality into space, and so on. In the main, we teach motor skills by initially putting the child through the movements so that he learns the required motor patterns. An accompanying concomitant to gross motor work is the child's increasing spontaneous imitative abilities. The specific types of activities we teach are those advocated by Kephart (1960). Swimming is an excellent supplement to a motor program and most autistic children genuinely enjoy it.

Other activities include visual training, arts and crafts, and music. As we mentioned earlier, many autistic children seem to have better peripheral than foveal vision, or at least they tend to use peripheral rather than central vision (Wing and Wing, 1971). They can be taught to use their eyes more efficiently and they need help in learning to move their eyes smoothly without accompanying head movements in order to follow a moving object visually. These are learned skills and hence, they can be taught. For visual training, we follow the procedures outlined by Kephart (1960).

Arts and crafts includes activities such as cutting with a scissors, pasting, painting, imprinting with a variety of materials, paper weaving, sewing and simple embroidery, measuring and ruling, coloring, patterning, clay modelling, mosaic tile-setting, leather stitching, and so on. Initially it is necessary to put the child through many of these activities, but in time he becomes able to take over the task on his own. Similarly with cutting, we teach scissors work by having the child use a four-ring scissors at the outset so that both the child and the adult can insert their fingers in the rings to facilitate guiding the child's hands through the motions of cutting. Among our objectives, in teaching arts and crafts, are improved eye-hand coordination and the development of work-orientation and prevocational skills.

Most autistic children enjoy music. Many of them learn to carry a tune at a very early age and usually they have a good sense of rhythm. This doesn't mean, however, that they are able to beat out a rhythm at the outset with either their hands or the rhythm band instruments, although they usually enjoy having us put them through it. Though several of our children can sing a song very readily by themselves, group singing is very difficult to accomplish as it takes a long time for the children to learn to sing along with others.

Among the educational devices that we use with some of our children is a Borg Warner System 80 teaching machine. It has been our experience that the children enjoy working with a teaching machine, and the programmed approach is very effective with most autistic children. However, some of the children have real difficulty in eye-hand coordination here: the child indicates the correct answer and aims at the appropriate key; but somehow the finger frequently lands to the right or the left of it. This tends to improve in time.

The typewriter, too, is a valuable teaching tool for a child whose eye-hand coordination is sufficiently developed. While the less severely afflicted child has little difficulty in learning the touch system and using the typewriter efficiently, it remains to be seen whether we can succeed in helping the more atypical child attain real speed and facility on the machine.

There are two other areas that we want to discuss briefly: We have already indicated the importance of self-care, self-help and socialization skills. Similarly, the teaching of work-orientation and of good work habits and attitudes should be an integral part of the child's curriculum from the very beginning of his school experience. Over and above this, we strongly advocate prevocational and vocational training, especially for older children; and a curriculum which emphasizes the building of work-related skills. Thus, some of the reading periods can focus on the reading of instructions for the use of a particular tool which the student would then use accordingly—a veridical Read and Do situation. An arithmetic lesson could center around the grouping of the required number of objects for an assembly task, etc. Teaching must, of course, be geared to the functional level of the specific child; within that framework, the youngster should learn the proper use of small hand tools, for instance, and then progress to power tools. Other possible activities would include assembly, packaging, sorting, collating, disassembly and envelope stuffing. Still other skills that might be taught include wood crafts, sanding and furniture refinishing, weaving, silk screening, light industrial work, building maintenance, grounds maintenance, homemaking skills and so on. In many instances, the successful teaching of these skills to autistic children will require a task-analysis approach: prior to the teaching of a specific skill, the teacher should prepare her lesson plan by beginning with the desired end product and then work backwards, analyzing the task step by step all the way back to its basic beginning. Then it can be taught to the child in this logical, sequential progression of small fundamental steps. Eventually, the school will build up a library of tested task-analyses for a great many specific work skills. Considerable creativity and ingenuity is required of the teaching staff in devising jigs and other equipment which will lead to increased student productivity and the elimination, to the greatest feasible extent, of the possibility of student errors. It's essential, too, that an incentive system of rewards be set up based on the amount of work the child does, how much supervision he requires, the quality of his work and so on.

We have not previously mentioned the necessity for a harmonious relationship between school and parents. This is vital. Unless there is close communication and coordination between home and school, the child's hopes for the future are minimized. He can make optimum progress only if he gets the same input at home that he gets at school. It's essential that the school provide guidance to the parents in the behavioral management of the child so that the youngster is handled with the same consistent approach on a 24-hour-a-day basis. Just as the professional staff is in control in the school situation, so the parents must learn the techniques of control in the home environment. Similarly, the parents must be kept informed of new skills the child acquires so that these can be incorporated into the child's day-to-day living at home. Parents should be notified particularly about the child's growth in speech so that they can reinforce it in the home by requiring the child to use his newly-acquired speech in appropriate situations. Still another area about which parents must be kept closely informed is the child's developing socialization and self-care skills. Otherwise, the parents will continue to help the youngster in self-care activities that the child has learned to perform independently at school. For example, one little boy learned, shortly after his school enrollment, how to unfasten and refasten his pants independently when he needed to go to the toilet. Nevertheless, he continued to let his parents perform this service for him at home until they accidentally learned some months later that he no longer needed their help. Obviously adequate communication between school and home, and between parents and school is a *must*. The benefits of the school program are maximized when parents and professionals act cooperatively.

We have not discussed materials *per se*, except in connection with the procedures described above. Of necessity, we make many of our own teaching materials, particularly for academic work, because we have to adapt them so our nonverbal autistic children can communicate to us what they are learning. In general, however, we see no inherent virtue in teacher-made materials if the commercial product is equally suitable. In other areas, we select materials because they have stimulus value to the eye and to the touch, because they teach valuable skills or concepts and/or because they are durable and attractive enough to perhaps capture the passing interest of a not-easily-motivated child.

Another area that we want to touch on briefly here is desirable teacher qualifications, characteristics and attitudes. In terms of training, we know of no school of education that has a program which is designed to train teachers of autistic children, particularly nonverbal autistic children. On that basis, an acceptable teacher should have a good background in either early childhood education or elementary education, supplemented by special education training and experience in teaching the emotionally disturbed child or the teaching of learning disabled children. However, as Wilson (1966) points out, ". . . no amount of reading about autistic children will give a clear idea of what they are like" (p. 179). Wilson describes the experience of a "highly skilled teacher" with "many years of outstanding service," who, because of her experience in teaching socially maladjusted children, was assigned to teach a class of young autistic children. According to Wilson, "After . . . three months she said that she had had to change all her ideas about how to approach these children. Nothing that she had learned earlier was any use to her" (p. 179). So, like Elgar (1966), we believe that ". . . there is no substitute for practical work with the children *under the guidance of an experienced teacher*" (p. 225) (italics ours).

In addition, the successful teacher of autistic children must be kind, and warm and generous with praise and affection when indicated. Simultaneously, he/she must be firm and demanding, and accepting but *not* patient (in terms of being resigned to bizarre, erratic and/or aggressive behavior and inattentiveness, based on the idea that "The child can't help it," rather than confronting the behavior and devising strategies to overcome it). The teacher must work toward extinguishing undesirable or socially unacceptable behaviors, but should not be personally disgusted by unappealing or unappetizing conduct, when it occurs; or feel threatened by tantrums. A good teacher is able to empathize, but *not* sympathize. Even though he understands how and why the child's multiple handicaps make bizarre mannerisms stimulating for the autistic youngster, he must nevertheless try to eliminate them from the child's behavioral repertoire. He/she must have the inner conviction that it is no kindness to autistic children, whether speaking or nonverbal, to permit them to vegetate rather than to demand performance. He must be convinced that it is a greater kindness to the child to give him a slap on his hand or on his bottom than it is to allow irrelevant responses or inattentiveness. He must be sufficiently secure about his value as a teacher that he can let the child know when he is angry, or frankly admit a mistake. He/she must be innovative and creative in devising and developing procedures which give the nonverbal or echolalic child an opportunity to demonstrate what *he* knows. Above all, the teacher must possess an attitude of confident expectancy: he should be "constantly testing to see whether the child has progressed sufficiently far to try something more complicated" (Wing and Wing, 1966, p. 196).

What we have described in this chapter is a behaviorally-oriented program and the teaching techniques it employs. In the sense that both mute and speaking autistic children *do* learn via these approaches, these are effective teaching methods, as the anecdotal reports and abbreviated case studies in the following chapter will attest. The logical next question is, do these procedures cure the children? And to that the answer, sadly, is no. But, to borrow Hewett's phrase (1970), they *do* make a difference. "No cure, but an unmistakable difference has occurred" (p. 53). And that "difference" presages the possibility of happier, more meaningful and more productive lives in adulthood for children who, without it, would be doomed to a lifetime in the back wards of an institution.

Chapter V

ANECDOTAL REPORTS: SEVEN AUTISTIC CHILDREN

T HE FOLLOWING ANDECDOTAL descriptions will illustrate some of the problems that autistic children present and the changes that occur in their functioning and behavior after they have been given a period of remedial education. The names of the children as listed below are not their own. With one exception which is so marked, the indicated age for each child is his/her age as of June, 1972.

Bill: Present age, 16 years, 11 months

When Bill was assigned to this teacher's class at midterm four and one-half years ago, he was a master of task avoidance. He seemed to be trying to find out, Will my new teacher be able to control me?, and he used every means at his disposal to test the situation. Testing for Bill included continuous and inappropriate giggling, refusal to focus his eyes on the presented lesson material, singing in an effort to drown out the teacher's voice, eating or mouthing the lesson materials and/or outright refusal to attend to the teacher or to perform. He was very hyperactive; and while he had some echolalic speech, he did not respond to questions addressed to him nor initiate or contribute in any way to a conversation. In terms of the possibility of evoking appropriate oral responses from him in the classroom, he had to be approached as though he were essentially nonverbal.

It took considerable persistence and insistence to develop cooperative behavior in Bill, but by June of 1968, just five months later, his year-end assessment reports:

> Bill has become almost a model student. The behavioral problems which were so much with us in February are now largely history. Once we upgraded the level of the work Bill

was required to do and conveyed to him that he was, indeed, *required* to do it, his motivation improved, and on the whole he has ceased to be a problem in the classroom. While he still requires a one-to-one relationship in order to do any academic work, he will do jigsaw puzzles, parquetry puzzles, and/or work with other materials very readily and independently when the teacher is occupied with another child.

His progress in academic areas has been amazing. While Bill's speech has improved somewhat this past term, he still has a major problem in verbalizing appropriately in situations where the speech that is required of him is dictated by external circumstances—such as reading aloud—as opposed to speech which he initiates spontaneously from within himself. There seems to be a problem of some kind which inhibits his ability to summon the appropriate words in an oral reading situation. For this reason, it was decided to discontinue oral reading for Bill, and instead we adapted his reading material in such a way that he could communicate to us via his selection from multiple choice responses, his comprehension and understanding of the material he was reading silently. Many of the answers from which he must choose consist of six-to-ten-word sentences and Bill's choices are almost invariably correct. There is no question but what he is reading them. His occasional incorrect responses stem from the fact that Bill has difficulty in sustaining a visual focus; but when, upon the teacher's insistence, he *looks,* Bill is able to select the correct answer. . . . He is making good progress in Level One arithmetic.

Bill has also been required to compose and write his own sentences in reply to questions we ask him related to his work. He has major difficulty with writing, and to do it at all, he needs the touch of the teacher's finger on his hand, very lightly— not guiding, but merely touching—to structure the task for him. Nevertheless, his choice of words and the composition of his sentences reveal the existence of a considerable reservoir of inner language. . . .

When Bill entered puberty, his behavior became extremely erratic once again. His attention span became much shorter and his behavior was marked by compulsive eating of both food and nonfood items. Brief intervals when he demonstrated good motivation were interrupted by an inability to sustain his attention on the proffered work material, even in a one-to-one teaching situation, and general acting-out behavior in the classroom. At that time, this teacher left the school where Bill was then enrolled and Bill was assigned to another teacher. Simultaneously, the orientation of the school changed from behavioral to analytical, with a concomitant permissive approach to the handling of the children. Bill's June, 1970, assessment says, "His concept development and general reasoning ability has been extremely limited, due to past classroom experiences which were extremely frustrating and unrealistic." At the close of the school year in June, 1971, his then-teacher reported,

> Academically, Bill's functioning is still at the pre-readiness level. He can identify the primary colors, . . . and is able to distinguish and identify simple shapes: square, circle, triangle, dog, cat, boy. . . . Bill has made no progress in academic areas this year: he is performing at the same level at year-end as he was at the beginning. . . . It seems that Bill is capable of learning only very simple tasks, and an unstructured, permissive environment seems to facilitate whatever learning does occur. . . . It was decided that very little should be asked of Bill in terms of traditional academics, and he seemed to be contented with the self-indulgence such a school environment afforded him. His teachers felt that it was unreasonable to attempt to teach him academic material. Instead, the permissive approach that was followed with him enabled him to satisfy some of his primitive needs with no fear of punishment. Bill was permitted to explore the classroom at will, occupying himself as he chose with whatever toys and materials were available. . . . Bill is a profoundly retarded adolescent whose severely limited capacities can best develop in a permissive setting that would provide him long term care and an opportunity to indulge himself as he wishes.

At that time, Bill's parents withdrew him from the school he had been attending, and in September, 1971, he was enrolled in The Rimland School for Autistic Children. The report of his initial functioning reads,

> Bill demonstrated his academic abilities only in brief flashes. He was very tense and uptight, and it took real persistence on his teachers' part to keep him at the task at hand. . . .
> It was difficult to equate the Bill who was so sure-footed and fleet when he raced downstairs to the kitchen for an unauthorized raid on the refrigerator with the Bill we saw

during gross motor work. . . . it was hard for him to execute
bodily movements on command. . . .

At the outset, Bill seemed to be smoldering. Behavioral
episodes were an almost daily occurrence.

The year-end report dated June, 1972, outlines Bill's
achievements in reading, writing and arithmetic, as well as in
speech, gross motor, manual manipulative and behavioral
areas. The assessment reads,

> Bill is reading in Book 2 of the Sullivan Programmed
> Readers; has completed all of the 50 units in Book A of the
> Following Directions Series; and once-weekly, reads a teacher-
> prepared sports story. Bill shows no problems with his reading
> and is making steady progress. . . . In writing, Bill has gained
> more control . . . at both desk and chalkboard, he can often
> write now for brief periods without requiring the touch of the
> teacher's finger on his hand, and he shows real pleasure in his
> success. . . . In Math, he is working with numerals up to 120,
> and with + and − problems involving the addition and/or
> subtraction of figures up to 4. He has also done some work in
> place value concepts. . . . In manual manipulative work, Bill
> will complete an entire task—such as a lacing card, or a
> "people" puzzle, or an intricate parquetry pattern, indepen-
> dently—frequently without needing so much as a reminder from
> one of his teachers to finish his work. . . . Gross motor work is
> still another area where Bill has shown improvement, . . . has
> greater control of his balance, and better coordination. . . Bill
> is doing more talking now—appropriately—than he was at the
> beginning of the school year. . . . His behavior, which was
> erratic and frequently unpredictable at the outset, has greatly
> improved. Now he has a longer attention span and greater con-
> trol. . . . He is more alert, motivation is better, and he has be-
> come much easier to work with . . . Socially, academically, and
> prevocationally, he is making gains.

Cathy: Present age, 16 years, 8 months

Most of Cathy's schooling had been in a day school for
retarded children, where her teachers confessed that she baf-
fled them, and her progress was nonexistent. During the year
just prior to her enrollment in The Rimland School, Cathy was
placed in a residential treatment center. They reported in
August, 1971,

. . . Cathy receives individual psychotherapy. Behavioral approach with punishment and reward was used in the unit with excellent results. Her adaptation and concentration improved, her initial hyperactivity disappeared, and she became more involved and aware of her environment. In January, 1971, she began to attend the nursery school for autistic children in our Children's Clinic. . . . She received special education which caused her to increase perceptual ability, improve and stimulate verbal and body expression, help her to differentiate herself from others, and enlarge and develop her abilities as much as possible in all areas. By the end of the year Cathy had made significant progress and it was felt at that point that she was ready to be placed in some kind of school setting where, under close supervision and . . . one to one or a very small teaching group, she would be able to develop more adaptive skills.

Cathy's abilities were at the preacademic or readiness level when she was enrolled in our school in September, 1971. She was extremely resistant to any task she was asked to do. She specialized in giving wrong answers—her forte was 100 percent error, which indicated that in actual fact, she knew and understood her lesson materials very well indeed! Though Cathy had considerable speech, none of it was communicative. She used a variety of devices to try to escape the presented task: her eyes focused everywhere except on the proffered materials; she would go into a long, echolalic monologue, which was totally unrelated to the on-going situation and so on. It developed that a slap on the hand, when Cathy persisted in deliberate errors, would cause her hand to literally *fly* to the correct answer! By this means, we ascertained that Cathy knew colors and color names, that she could associate the name of an object with its pictured representation and that she could select the appropriate picture from among a multiple-choice grouping on the basis of a description of its function. In the motor area she had some spastic movements and some equilibrium problems. However, she could perform both volitionally and on command though she was slow in her responses. Behavior-wise, her aloneness was striking. She did not like to be touched and tended to move away from people. Though she was capable of well-articulated speech, she did not reply to questions and her speech was echolalic, not conversational. Her resistance was quiet but extremely persistent. Once she had given a single correct response during a lesson period, her attitude indicated that she had sufficiently rewarded her teacher so the teacher should kindly take this as a cue to end the lesson and go away! She did nothing at all except during her one-to-one tutorial periods with a teacher. The rest of the time she totally ignored the work she was given to do on her own. Seemingly, what she preferred to do was to sit at her desk doing nothing.

Her year-end progress report, dated June, 1972, reads,

. . . Cathy's prereading and reading readiness activities have followed a steady progression to increasingly more complex tasks. These have included: matching pictures; categorizing, by selecting from among a multiple choice grouping, the two pictures that go together, such as a cup and a saucer; or selecting the one picture that *doesn't* belong in a multiple choice grouping—such as the picture of a food among a grouping of pictures of various kinds of furniture; matching letters of the alphabet; matching the letters of a word; matching pairs of words; and so on. Cathy can now read simple words, and match them with the appropriate picture. Moreover, her accompanying verbalization is appropriate. She shows good comprehension of picture stories.

Though she had a major problem in controlling a pencil at the outset of the school year, she can now write letters and simple words.

She has completed 63 pages of her mathematics workbook (Level One), where she is working on problems involving quantities up to 10 + 1, and numerals up to 11, and understands these concepts, both abstractly and concretely. There are days when she shows a real interest in math, and works diligently. She has become increasingly motivated and cooperative. This is not intended to imply that Cathy's negativism is now a thing of the past—it is still frequently in evidence. But there has been a considerable change from the *consistent* negativism and resistance to *every* presented task to her present much-more-than-occasional interest and usually good performance. She now does some independent seatwork without direct teacher supervision in both reading and math. She is able to do good work with manual manipulative materials, but she does virtually nothing in this area unless her teacher works with her in a one-to-one situation.

She participates well in the circle games and other activities of our daily game period. There has been some improvement in Cathy's use of speech for communication: she replies to questions some of the time and occasionally volunteers a bit of information. There is greater spontaneity in her functioning; she is much more responsive than she was initially. She has recently begun to initiate approaches to her teachers.

In general, she is more in contact with her environment these days. Cathy has much more abiltiy than she is willing to reveal. Nevertheless, she has made definite progress in both cognitive and performance areas, and she has crossed the threshold into the beginnings of academic work.

Donald: Present age, 17 years, 7 months

Don learned to read and write long before he developed speech. A 1965 report describes him at age ten and one-half:

Though Don has no speech, he displays exceptional ability in academic areas. In a highly structured situation where there is a one-to-one relationship, he reads, writes, and does arithmetic at levels considerably beyond his chronological age. Though he has no apparent motor disability, his control of the pencil is poor, he writes quite slowly, and his handwriting is large, poorly formed, and immature for his age. Nevertheless, he has a tremendous written vocabulary, is an excellent speller, and can express himself fluently in writing. His written expressions are always appropriate to the situation, meaningful, and intelligent.

Don reads very rapidly and seems able to take in a whole paragraph or more at a glance. He never reads for amusement, however; he reads only when a teacher presents a book to him during a lesson period.

In the area of mathematics, particularly, Don seems remarkably able. He can do relatively complex math problems—square root, algebra problems in two unknowns, problems in bases other than 10, *et cetera*—mentally, as easily as with pencil and paper.

However, virtually *none* of these abilities is apparent in Don's general functioning, which is very atypical, and in the main, considerably below his chronological age. Although he is normal in appearance, his behavior is definitely not that of a normal child. His play habits are limited in variety, and at best, very immature for his age. He never *elects* academic-type activity of his own volition: though he does this, at times willingly, at others unwillingly during lesson periods, he *never* chooses an activity of this nature when left to his own devices. He has great difficulty in finding constructive ways in which to spend his free time.

At the time of his initial school enrollment at the age of six and one-half, Don was already doing academic work. Two months after his enrollment, the school reported,

> Don demonstrated all the skills his mother had demonstrated for us and then went way beyond. In the area of abstractive abilities, we finally cut off testing on the high school level without feeling we had yet reached a definite ceiling. In manipulating concrete situations, he showed a very spotty scale of achievement but the ability to learn readily when his negative defenses were penetrated.
>
> For example, he has learned to play and use dominoes and is beginning to understand and show skill in the use of the Stern program of structural arithemetic. Yet, he was able to solve problems in probability in a second year high school algebra book.
>
> Likewise, Don shows great ability to understand stories and material on very high levels of achievement in reading. He can answer abstract questions about the stories. To date we have not been able to test his concrete understandings of these stories.

Don attended this school for four years, during which there was virtually no continuity in curriculum or programming, frequent teacher turnover, and a generally inconsistent educational orientation.

In 1965, and again in 1966, Don's parents brought him to see Dr. Ivar Lovaas at the University of California in Los Angeles, for two separate ten-day visits. Here Dr. Lovaas' staff taught Don's mother the methods they used in developing speech in nonverbal autistic children. As a result of his mother's subsequent work with Don at home, he developed some speech. It was very poor in quality and articulation, and Don rarely initiated a conversation, but now he was able to answer questions orally and to verbalize his needs and wants.

Another change in Don's life at that time was that his parents enrolled him in a different day school in September, 1965. But their hopes that his new school situation would provide positive programming proved unfounded. In this school, too, there was a succession of teachers in the classroom to which Don was assigned, none of whom knew how to establish effective control over their autistic students, so that no constructive teaching program developed. In 1968, this teacher was employed by Don's new school; and for the following two years, Don had an effective program of remedial education.

His 1970 progress report reads, in part:

> Don is able to read the eighth grade level material presented to him with no difficulty, and replies orally to questions put to him by the teacher about the meaning of what he has read, word definitions, and so on. Another reading activity, "Read and Do", involves his reading the instructions printed on a 3 × 5 inch index card, and then doing it. The instructions are at two levels of difficulty: a single command, such as "Pull up the window shade"; and a sequence of two instructions, such as "Jump two times, and then clap your hands once." Don has difficulty in following more than one command at a time, and with the two-sequence instructions, the teacher usually has to say something like "And then, what?" after Don has completed the first part of the sequence, before he then moves into following the second instruction. . . .
>
> Don's writing at the chalkboard shows considerable improvement. It is still very large: his letters are about eight inches tall—but he is usually conscientious in his efforts to form his letters well. He writes with the teacher's hand at the back of his head. . . . At his desk, he writes with no manual contact with the teacher, but his control of the pencil is still very poor and the teacher usually provides a "bumper" to help him stay within his lines. . . . The quality of the content of what he writes is good. . . .
>
> Don is very quick at grasping abstract arithmetical concepts. . . . His work in arithmetic has been largely in a 7th grade accelerated series, which we hope will fill in some of the gaps that may have occurred because of the inconsistent teaching program he has had in the past. He is doing very good work.
>
> Don is not particularly interested, or too cooperative, in doing simple manual manipulative activities which he is given to do on his own. He does very little, unless he has one-to-one supervision. . . .

Behaviorally, Don averages about one screaming tantrum per week. We are unable to attribute this tantrum behavior to a specific cause. This is a long-standing behavioral pattern with Don, dating back some years; and none of the measures we have used has been successful in eliminating it. . . .

In the main, provided his teacher is working directly with him, Don is attentive, responsive, cooperative, and interested in the work materials.

This teacher left the school's faculty at that time, and simultaneously, the orientation of the program changed from behavioral and demanding, to analytical and permissive. The change in Don's functioning, after a year of this new regime, is striking. His 1971 report reads,

Don displays little ability to conceptualize or use reasoning ability. . . . If the task required is at a low enough level for Don, his performance will benefit. . . . All chalkboard work must be limited to less than one minute. . . . Because of Don's conceptual deficits, the differentiation between perceptual and conceptual deficits cannot be clearly or completely stated or observed. . . . A way must be found to help Don control his behavior. . . .

In September, 1971, Don's parents enrolled him in the then-newly-founded Rimland School. In June, 1972, his teacher reports,

Don's academic abilities seem to suggest a potential at at least the twelfth grade level. However, his dependence on individual teacher attention and the practical limitations on the amount of teacher time that can be devoted to him, slows him down to a lower level of academic functioning. . . . His written answers to the exercises which accompany his reading material are original, and show good insight and wit. . . . There is a major discrepancy between the quality of the content of his writing, which is commensurate with the level of his good academic abilities, and the generally poor quality of the letter formations in the actual writing itself. . . . He has been introduced to the touch system of typing; but he types very slowly, and insists on being touched while he is typing. This touching was then withheld . . . before he was willing to accept it. The resultant frustration he builds up during a typing session sometimes erupts into a behavioral episode. . . . Don grasps mathematics concepts very quickly. He is able to compute mentally, and can both give rapid answers, and explain his methods. . . . Regarding his independent seatwork in reading and math, . . . it has to be understood that working independently, without teacher supervision, is a major hurdle for Don. While the results achieved thus far in this area are less than spectacular, each instance is nevertheless "monumental."

Don demonstrates some good gross motor abilities, but they are not always at his command. . . .

In the area of manual manipulative abilities, Don has improved—not so much in his ability to handle the materials, which we know he can do, since the work is well within his range of abilities, but in his *willingness* to do. In recent months there have been a growing number of occasions when he has made a genuine attempt to do his work on his own. However, too often still, the work remains on his desk either untouched or merely fiddled with. . . .

He requires one-to-one teacher attention for most of his work in the arts and crafts area. . . .

. . . Don initiates very little speech. He is presently in a phase of verbally confirming his activities by telling us—repeatedly and perseveratively—what he has just done, which may very well stem from a primitive attempt at conversation. However, his articulation is very poor. He can "clean up" his articulation to some extent, but it requires major effort on his part. When he talks . . . he uses a one-word-at-a-time delivery, and his voice is virtually devoid of inflection. He also has poor control over the volume of his voice so that it is frequently much too loud. . . .

There are days, and even weeks, when Don is affable and pleasant. At other times, there seems to be an incipient tantrum brewing all day long. . . . Depending on his mood, it is possible at times to "josh" him out of a threatening behavioral outburst. . . . In general, these behavioral episodes have become less frequent; and when they do occur, they are much briefer in duration. . . .

Don must be helped to develop greater independence of performance . . .

Fred: Present age, 15 years, 9 months

Fred received individual psychotherapy on an outpatient basis from the age of five and one-half until he was nearly nine years old. During 14 months of that period, his therapist utilized a combination of human operant conditioning techniques along the lines developed by Ferster (1961) in his work with autistic children, and traditional psychotherapeutic techniques, in an effort to develop speech in this nonverbal child. At the end of that time, Fred was much less withdrawn than he had been at the outset of treatment; he had become much less inhibited about exploring his environment and "spontaneously toilet trained himself . . . Deliberate efforts to produce speech were discontinued" after 14 months. "The effort seemed to be substantially unproductive and was inducing more frustration in both therapist and patient than seemed desirable." The 1965 report continues,

> Fred still uses almost no understandable expressive speech. He can communicate "yes" and "no" through the use of consistent but idiosyncratic sounds. For about two months he has been babbling a good deal with apparent wish to communicate; melody of speech is present. When his babbling is not understood, Fred displays impatience and continues his efforts at communication. Receptive speech is quite good. Fred seems to understand nearly everything that is said to him and ordinarily responds in an appropriate fashion. Response breakdown occurs when the communication includes a request for some bodily action. He seems to have difficulty translating word input into muscle output and such output usually must be gesturally demonstrated before it is accomplished the first time.
>
> Fred is an active and agile boy. . . . His former constriction and rigidity are not observed; his ineptness with his hands is less marked but he still resists learning manual skills. . . . He can scribble with pencil and crayon but will not copy forms unless his hand is firmly held.
>
> Fred seems to be a happier child than he used to be. . . . He teases in a playful manner. Fred communicates negative feelings vocally but has not panicked for several months. Even firm, irritated words from the therapist fail to provoke panic or withdrawal. Fred rarely expresses aggressive feelings; . . . he has never struck, kicked, or bit even when being forced to undergo painful examinations when he was ill.
>
> Fred is no longer withdrawn from peers or adults. . . . He can maintain good eye contact and does when spoken to or when he is attempting to communicate . . .
>
> Fred has been accepted in a suitable school . . . so his case will be closed here. . . .

At the age of nine, Fred was enrolled in a day care center for retarded children. Six years later, in 1971, the day care center reported,

> Fred had no previous school record when he entered our Center. He was a very shy, scared nine-year-old boy. He was frightened of strange places and strange people.
>
> His behavior was always good, but he would not take any type of changes. Such as changing in different rooms, different size buses, or teachers. When he entered, he could not stand loud noises.
>
> Fred did very little academic work. He put little effort in working with his hands. All his work was at a kindergarten level.

In September, 1971, Fred was enrolled in The Rimland School. Informal testing at that time revealed,

> Fred was performing on a preacademic level at the time of his enrollment. He has no speech, but he does have a definitive point. He was able to identify colors by pointing to the appropriate color when the examiner asked for them by name. He could identify objects, and/or pictures, by pointing correctly to whichever one the examiner named. He was able to do some categorizing: when the examiner set before him two related items plus a picture of a third unrelated item, Fred could point correctly in response to the question, "Which one doesn't belong?" He could reproduce simple block patterns, but he insisted on doing them *on top* of the pictured pattern rather than alongside of it. He needed some help in arranging picture stories in sequence. He seemed unable to grasp the idea of rhyming so that with neither objects nor pictures was he able to point to the two items whose names rhymed, not even when the examiner named each item for him orally. His motor performance indicated an overall lack of good coordination.

In general, Fred's performance showed that he had both the readiness, and more importantly, the willingness, to move ahead to work at a higher cognitive level. The reports we had received from his previous school placement had indicated a lower level of performance than we were able to evoke from him in our preliminary testing. Fred was obviously capable of a higher level of performance than he had previously demonstrated. Perhaps his docile nature had merely won him anonymity in the much-less-favorable staff-child ratio classroom which constituted his school experience prior to his enrollment with us.

His June, 1972 year-end assessment reports,

Fred is now able to read simple words on sight, and match them with the appropriate picture. He can select the appropriate consonant letter from among a multiple choice grouping as the initial sound of a dictated word; he's able to select pictures whose names rhyme from among a multiple choice grouping: Fred no longer has any difficulty with rhyming; he has mastered concepts of size and of position, *et cetera*. He demonstrated a quick grasp of the concepts involved in all of his prereading and reading readiness activities.

Fred exhibits a great dependence on patterns or prompts. Because of the accuracy of his performance when prompts are withheld, we know that this does not stem from an inability to do the work; instead, the problem seems to lie in his desire to avoid the sole responsibility for his actions.

With the System 80 teaching machine, it has been very gratifying to see Fred grow from his initial pattern of dependency and requests for teacher confirmation of the accuracy of his choice before he could bring himself to depress the button, to independent performance and sure, quick choices by the end of the school year. He has completed all of Kits A and B which involve recognition of the capital and small letters of the alphabet. Fred did extremely well with these, and the self-confidence of his performance was a joy to behold. His performance with Kit C, which involves phonics and letter sounds, is so far less consistent . . . he seems to have some basic underlying difficulty with the auditory discrimination of letter sounds . . .

In writing activities, Fred has made consistent gains. At the beginning of the school year, Fred could not control either pencil or chalk. Now, with a model to copy from, he is able to reproduce geometrical forms, numerals, and letters quite faithfully, with or without direct teacher supervision. . . . When he's asked to draw a form, or write a letter or a numeral from memory, however, he's unable to do it at times—though he's improving somewhat in this regard.

Fred's consistent love has been math. This has been his easiest subject. His grasp of both abstract and concrete concepts is good, and on a par. He learns fast in this area and retains the concepts he learns. Fred needs only a simple explanation from the teacher; then he can take over on his own and complete the written work required to do one or two pages of his math workbook on his own without teacher supervision. Math is intrinsically rewarding for Fred, and he will work independently here without requiring concrete rewards to motivate him.

He has made phenomenal progress in his work with manual manipulative materials. He can now handle all of our manipulative materials with ease on his own. This has been built up gradually, and required considerable one-to-one help for a number of months. It is as though we have watched Fred master his hands.

In the gross motor area, Fred has gained more control of his larger muscles. His movements are less erratic, but they are still not entirely at his command.

Fred is a joiner. He needs no reminder to stay with the group during our daily game period. He imitates the other children's movements very readily when this is required, and when it's his turn to lead the other children in a motion of some kind for them to copy, he's very creative and spontaneous about offering new motions.

Fred still has no speech, but his voice has good intonation and inflection when he makes a series of sounds as he tries to communicate and the number of sounds he makes for any given word corresponds exactly with the number of syllables in the word. The result is that Fred is able to communicate very well in an in-context situation by means of sounds and some gestures. He dislikes being asked to reproduce specific sounds but he does try to do this on request at least some of the time; we have succeeded in getting some imitative sounds and an occasional word from him now and again.

Fred combines contradictory qualities: he is warm, friendly and perceptive with his teachers, but with his classmates he maintains a distance, though he's very aware of what they're doing and shows some insight about their behavior.

Behaviorally, Fred continues to be good-natured and cooperative. He loves to be praised, enjoys his tangible rewards and has a good sense of humor. He still tries at times to function below his abilities.

On the whole, Fred is a good student and a joy to have in the classroom. He has made great gains in cognitive areas this past year and he himself takes pride in his steady growth and achievement.

Jack: Present age, 9 years, 1 month

Jack was enrolled in The Rimland School in January, 1972. For three and one-half years prior to his enrollment with us, he had had residential placement in a speech training program. As of December, 1971, the Institute reported,

> At the time of termination there was considerable babbling heard. Occasionally a one-word response or a two-word phrase was heard. Jack was able to follow through on simple, one-part verbal requests or commands. He would come when called. He preferred to mouth everything given to him, although with close supervision this could be inhibited. Autistic-type behaviors such as bending at the waist and touching the floor continued to be observed.
>
> Jack continued to take himself to the bathroom as needed. He slept soundly throughout the night. Self-feeding and acceptance of a wide variety of foods demonstrated marked improvement, if offered no alternative. Undressing and dressing skills were adequate with the exception of tying shoe laces. With an interested adult close by, Jack would engage in constructive play activities as: stringing beads, placing forms in a tupperware ball, working wooden puzzles and putting pegs in a pegboard. During this reporting period, progress has been observed in the following two areas: picture identification and touching or pointing to facial parts on command. Progress continues to be slow in color matching and verbal production. The insight shown in color matching in one speech session may be absent in a subsequent session. Jack can identify objects and pictures by indicating the correct one when they are named. One-to-one supervision is required to keep Jack on a task long enough to complete it. In physical education, Jack's attention span remains short, and his general level of cooperative behavior within a group setting as this is poor. His competitive behaviors, as in racing, are low. For these reasons Jack requires much individual attention with manual manipulation. He can imitate gross motor movements as clapping hands, hands over head, "spinning," marching, etc., but does not always do so.
>
> Jack says water, cookie, bye and hi. Otherwise he will lead an adult by the hand to his want or need. If requests contrary to his wishes are made of him he becomes aggressive to the point of hitting, biting or scratching. However, for the most part he is happy and smiling.

Our own early evaluative procedures with Jack established the fact that he could match colors and knew color names. Similarly, we ascertained that he could match geometrical forms correctly, and in a very short space of time he was able to associate the name of a form with the appropriate geometrical shape. However, we discovered that Jack is a master of escape, and we think this accounts for some of the inconsistencies of performance reported by the Institute as well as the discrepancies between our findings and theirs. At The Rimland School we insisted that Jack perform as directed and our persistence was rewarded by the discovery that Jack had already acquired considerable knowledge in preacademic areas, most of which was not apparent in terms of the mere observation of his general functioning.

Our year-end report in June, 1972 reads,

> Jack progressed rapidly through increasingly complex pre-reading and reading readiness activities and is now able to read simple words and match them with the appropriate object or picture. He has acquired some simple phonics skills and can designate the consonant letter which is the initial sound of either a dictated word or of the name of a picture. He demonstrates good comprehension of picture stories, and even with the book closed can replicate positions of characters, objects and colors.

> At both desk and chalkboard, he can now make a circle, a cross and an X on his own, and he will attempt a square and a triangle following verbal directions. He is also tracing letters and doing so with interest.

> In math Jack understands concepts of more, less and equal, and is now working with quantities up to ten. He knows, and can correctly identify, numerals up to ten and is able to assign the appropriate numeral to a pictured group of objects and/or to associate the appropriate number of pictured objects in a set or of concrete objects placed before him with the correct numeral—all with no difficulty once he becomes convinced that tears or a tantrum will not win him release from the task at hand. He needs additional work in concretizing his numbers concepts.

> In both the reading and math areas, he completes a daily worksheet independently with no direct teacher supervision. The worksheet requires him to fasten the correct answer in the appropriate space or "box" on the sheet below the presented reading or math problem. We're very pleased with Jack's growth in this area of independent seatwork. When he entered the program in January, his attention span was so short and unsustained that he required one-to-one teacher attention for the completion of any task. This is still largely true. Neverthe-

less, he is now frequently completing these four-part and sometimes five-part worksheets (which we admittedly give him in the smallest possible increments) independently, or with minimal teacher supervision. Moreover, this work is at a considerably higher cognitive level than anything Jack had ever done prior to his enrollment in our program.

In manual manipulative areas, Jack can do intricate work with his hands. This is best seen in the rituals he goes through with strings, beads, pegs, jigsaw puzzles, *et cetera*—in preference to doing these tasks as they are intended to be done. He *is* able to perform these tasks properly: an oral reminder from one of his teachers to "Get on with your work" will result in his stringing another bead or placing another puzzle piece. But he shows very little goal-persistence or motivation here and usually returns to his own rituals in very short order, continuing the task again only momentarily each time one of his teachers admonishes him. Given direct teacher supervision, Jack is able to complete most of these tasks quickly and easily.

Jack now understands much more readily than he did at first what we are asking him to do in various exercises and games during the gross motor and game periods. He can now do some of these activities on his own without teacher assistance. For others, he now actively seeks teacher help in being put through an activity rather than the seeming obliviousness to the ongoing exercise that he exhibited at first. In the main, however, Jack requires a one-to-one relationship for most motor activities.

Under direction, Jack can handle a scissors fairly well, paste, color and so on, but he does not work independently and requires one-to-one teacher attention in order to perform.

Speechwise, we have not yet been able to increase Jack's four-word vocabulary. We have been successful in getting him to imitate sounds and sometimes words on occasion.

Jack is affectionate and aware. He runs less these days. He can sit for longer periods. He continues to tease, but not as unremittingly as at first. He follows directions better, though he does so at his own speed. The resistance to lessons has diminished and his biting and scratching are much less in evidence.

Considering that Jack is only intermittently motivated by primary reinforcers, and shows few overt signs of being pleased by praise, we feel that we have experienced considerable success in the brief six-month-period of his enrollment with us in uncovering and developing some of his previously latent abilities.

Steve: Age, at time of June, 1969 report, 11 years, 6 months

Steve was admitted to this teacher's classroom in 1968 just two months before the end of the school year. For several years prior, he had been enrolled in a school for retarded children. On admission, he was so hypoactive and lethargic that he seemed almost catatonic. He was totally nonverbal; and completely oblivious of oral commands, particularly at those times when he was on his feet and in motion. Even when he was seated, however, and the command required him to get to his feet, it was necessary to repeat it several times with increasing emphasis, thus: "Steve, up! UP, Steve! *UP!*", accompanied by vigorous illustrative arm motions to indicate what was required of him before Steve would become activated. It took considerable effort initially to elicit performance from him, but once the ice was broken, he demonstrated that he could sort colors, knew color names, could match geometrical forms and, with considerable prodding, could then point to the "circle," the "square," the "cross," *et cetera* so that it became obvious he had made the association between the name of the form and its geometrical shape. It further developed, and this was surprising in the light of Steve's general immobility, that he was able to do simple jigsaw puzzles independently without structuring at those times when his teachers were occupied with other children. Steve was highly motivated by food, and primary reinforcement, such as M&M candies, proved very effective in working with him.

His year-end progress evaluation, in June, 1968, reads,

. . . Prereading and reading readiness activities have included matching pictures, matching letters of the alphabet, matching words to pictures and/or to the appropriate objects and so on. Steve is able to find the two matching words from among a group of five words, and he is almost invariably accurate. A vital prerequisite to any of these activities is that Steve must be required to *look,* both during the process of examining the materials that have been offered to him and also while he is indicating his answers.

Another reading readiness activity is the use of a prereading workbook. Since Steve is nonverbal, we have adapted the material in this workbook to enable Steve to demonstrate how well he is able to grasp the lessons involved. Thus, for picture stories, for example, Steve is required to select the appropriate answer to the questions we put to him from among a group of possible answers we have prepared. We have Steve show us which panel in the picture story we are talking about, then put the questions to him. He selects from the multiple choice answers, each printed on a separate card, in one of two ways: where the answer involved is longer than three or four words, we read each of the possible choices aloud to Steve, making sure that he knows what each card says. Steve must then point to the card with the correct answer on it. Where the answer in question is brief—three words or less—we first give Steve an opportunity to read it himself. At least some of the time he is able to do this. Steve, astoundingly, is already doing some reading, though this skill is not really well established as yet. His answers to the questions about the stories indicate that his comprehension is good.

Steve is also required to spell simple, one-syllable dictated words using link-letters; and he does very well with this. He also does well when we present him with a group of about five words from which he must choose the word we want after we tell him what the word means.

Writing practice at this time consists of guided developmental writing and/or tracing in clay, on paper and on the chalkboard. Steve does not yet control the pencil and/or chalk well enough to be able to function without teacher assistance here. This is an area in which he needs considerable work—as well as in the development of other fine motor skills. In pegboard activities, for instance, Steve handles the pegs quite awkwardly.

He is making good progress in his Level One arithmetic workbook, and shows a good grasp of basic numbers concepts up to five.

Gross motor-wise, Steve is improving somewhat in his ability to obey commands, although so far this is a slow process. Steve needs to do a great deal of gross motor work.

There is still no speech at this time.

In manual manipulative areas, Steve is performing simple tasks like jigsaw puzzles, nesting cups or clipping clothespins independently without direct teacher supervision.

Considering that Steve has been in attendance for less than two months, we feel that he has made very good progress. Much of the work that he is presently doing is at a considerably higher intellectual level than he has ever before been exposed to, and his response to it is very gratifying.

When school opened the following September, Steve demonstrated that he had retained what he had learned during his prior period of attendance. He continued to make steady progress. He was withdrawn from the program at the end of the school year in June, 1969, because his father was transferred to a job in another state. At that time, his teacher described his status thus:

> . . . Steve is not a behavior problem in the classroom. At the beginning of the school term it was necessary to intrude very insistently on Steve's disinterest and withdrawal in order to get him to attend to the task at hand. At no time was there tantrum behavior or any kind of loud outburst. He habitually displays a great many autistic mannerisms: finger play, head shaking, head banging, etc.
>
> Steve relates better to adults than he does to other children. On the first day of school, a kind of shy smile communicated his pleasure at returning to school. We feel that he enjoys being with the other children, but he makes no overtures to them.
>
> The three multiple-choice answers from which Steve must choose during his work with picture stories now consist of six-to-ten-or-twelve-word sentences and Steve's selections are usually quick and definitive. We don't know whether he is, in fact, reading every word of these sentences, but he *is* reading enough to be able to select the appropriate answer. He is doing equally good work in his Level One programmed reader.
>
> Steve's control of the pencil and of chalk is improving though he will continue to need additional work in this area for some time to come. Nevertheless, he is now able to give one-word replies in writing to questions put to him by his teacher, or name in writing either an actual object or a pictured object or write a word that rhymes with a word said by the teacher. For most of this writing he requires the touch of the teacher's index finger, not guiding, but just barely touching his writing hand. Occasionally however, he is able to write part or all of a word without requiring this manual contact. When he is given paper and pencil and told to practice writing on his own, Steve may make some dots and a few short lines on the paper, but his effort is something less than diligent. Occasionally, we require him to trace rhythmic writing patterns such as ocean

waves, overs, unders and so on, on either paper or chalkboard. Steve's tracing is not too exact, but he *will* do this without help or manual contact when he is supervised. On his own, however, he makes only a minimal attempt to follow the pattern and ceases all effort in very short order.

Steve usually enjoys arithmetic and is able to do simple plus and minus problems involving various combinations of numbers from one through nine both concretely and by selecting the appropriate numeral from among a group of possible answers. While he can tell very readily how many members there are in a group, he is not consistent in laying out *just* the number of concrete objects that are required in a given situation. We think this may stem from a problem in stopping, but it nevertheless indicates that he needs further work in concretizing his mathematical concepts.

Steve is gaining skill with the clay tray activities, and is increasing his ability to perform the finger and wrist exercises without help from the teacher. We have also been having him work on finger differentiation by having him play some notes on the piano for a few minutes several times a week. Steve can handle scissors well, but he has not yet learned to turn the paper properly by himself when cutting out a specific form. Neither can he follow the lines precisely enough when he is asked to cut along straight lines.

During our daily game period, Steve shows somewhat improved ability to participate. He is beginning to develop some rudimentary imitative behavior although it is still necessary to put him through many of the movements of the games. However, he occasionally hits the balloon across the table during a game of balloon volleyball, and he shows some slight improvement in his ability to sustain a visual focus during eye training —for example, when he is required to strike a hanging ball (suspended from the ceiling by a string) with a stick. In gross motor training, he still needs a great deal of work although he is considerably more mobile than he was at the beginning of the year.

Steve is being taught to button and unbutton, lace and tie a shoe, buckle and unbuckle a belt, fasten his trousers and so on. He removes and puts on his own jacket and/or sweater and he is able to fasten together and zip his jacket zipper with no help.

Perhaps the most promising development is that Steve has begun to use imitative speech during his daily speech therapy periods. In the classroom we do not hear much speech from him, but he has changed from an almost completely silent child to one who makes frequent speech sounds. On one occasion, when he was shown a ball so that he could write the appropriate word on the chalkboard, he not only wrote the word "ball" correctly, he also said "ball" orally.

Steve has improved in his ability to listen, but he needs a great deal of work in this area. At the beginning of the school term Steve *never* came when he was called unless the calling of his name was accompanied by a vigorous illustrative gesture. Now he will come at least some of the time solely on the strength of hearing his name called.

On the whole, Steve has improved in virtually every area of his functioning. He is much more "with it" now than he was at the outset of the school term. He teases on occasion. For instance when his name is called, he will pretend that he is ignoring it; and he doesn't come, so in a sense he *is* ignoring it. But he will sit there with a mischievous grin on his face which indicates that he is fully aware of the situation. Steve is a charming child; it is impossible to work with him on a daily basis without becoming aware of how appealing he is beneath his impersonal facade. His primary needs continue to be in motor, visual, speech and listening areas. It is hoped that he will continue to forge ahead in his new school situation.

Tony: Present age, 13 years, 9 months

Tony was enrolled in The Rimland School in September, 1971. His prior educational experience included some nine years of school placement in a number of different programs, both day and residential, most of them analytically-oriented.

Upon admission, he was almost totally negativistic. There was virtually no activity in which he cooperated willingly. His chief concern was the gratification of his own wishes; for example, he would swoop down on one of his classmates, pull a lollipop from the child's mouth, pop it into his own and chew it up so swiftly that even a nearby attending adult could not intervene to prevent it. He was oblivious of both the victim's outcry (if there was one—sometimes the other child remained impassive) and the slap on his hand and the oral disapproval of his teachers.

Tony was totally nonverbal. His preferred activity was to sit with his chair pushed back from his desk, one leg crossed over the other at the thigh, while he either twiddled some minute object, chewed (and sometimes swallowed) his work materials or picked away with his fingernails at the presented materials until he had succeeded in destroying them. He appeared content for the most part during these intervals, providing no one admonished him to get on with his work. At any moment, though, whether free or under pressure to perform, he could go into a rage reaction during which he would strike himself on the head repeatedly.

It was during his periods of individual work on a one-to-one basis with a teacher, however, that Tony demonstrated his mastery of the fine art of resistance. His immediate response, when a teacher approached him for a lesson period, was to jump up and run to the toilet. Investigation revealed that he did, in fact, urinate each time that he ran out of the classroom in this abrupt fashion. So, even though his timing was suspect, and despite the fact that at the beginning of the term he was urinating some 20 or more times daily during school hours, the staff accepted this as a legitimate need at the outset and we permitted it. Promptly upon Tony's return to the classroom, the teacher would attempt to go on with his lesson. Tony's reaction was to attack the teacher: he would grasp a part of the teacher's clothing in his fist, twisting it until it was in imminent danger of tearing; simultaneously, he pinched, bit and/or scratched the teacher's arms and hands until he drew blood. If the teacher persisted in continuing the lesson, Tony then attacked himself, slapping away at his head repeatedly unless he was restrained. Throughout these encounters, Tony cried loudly. When the tantrum was over and Tony was brought back to the task, he resisted in other ways: he persistently turned his head away so that he could not see the proffered materials; he wriggled his hands so that it was virtually impossible to put him through the task; during motor activities and games when he was required to stand up, he would either drop to the floor, or, if an attempt was being made to put him through a procedure, he would let his body grow limp so that he seemingly couldn't stand without adult support; and so on.

In terms of performance, despite Tony's massive resistance, it was determined that he could match colors and forms and associate the appropriate color and form with its name. He was able to select the appropriate noun picture from among a multiple choice grouping when it was asked for by name. These appeared to be the extent of his abilities in preacademic areas at the outset of the year. His control of both pencil and chalk was poor, and he could not be given a crayon for coloring in an unsupervised situation because he ate the crayon. He was adept at bead-stringing, simple puzzles and formboards, and could perceive elementary spatial relationships. He needed help when using scissors. In gross motor areas he was fairly well coordinated, but had no imitative behavior.

A major objective for Tony was to eliminate, or at least lessen the frequency of, his tantrums and self-mutilative behavior. He was told whenever he resisted a task, "In this school, you must do what you're told to do." The teacher would continue to work with him, ignoring Tony's loud wailing and his tears, and would put him through the task by manipulating Tony's hands if necessary, despite the fact that Tony was attempting to (successfully, much of the time) bite, pinch and scratch. We were very persistent; when Tony turned his head away, we held his chin with one hand and forced him to *look* at the work materials. When he wriggled his hands (during writing exercises, for example), we tightened our grip on his hand and put him through the activity and so on. Though all three of Tony's teachers have scars to show for their efforts, Tony was *never* permitted to escape a task by going into a tantrum or by resisting it physically. Whenever he pinched or scratched, he was slapped on the hand and told *"No!"* When he bit, he was slapped lightly on the mouth and told, *"No!"* Successful performance and/or the merest attempt at cooperative behavior were always rewarded with an M&M and lavish praise and affection. The one thing we would not tolerate was Tony's hitting himself. As soon as he began this kind of behavior, we would attempt to stop it with a loud, firm "NO!", and when this proved ineffective (as it always did at the outset), Tony's hands were tied so that he could not continue to strike himself. This of course interrupted the task and the teacher then always made it a point to move on to the next child for individual work, ignoring Tony completely, despite his loud wailing. Tony resented this, and would sometimes try to interject himself physically between the teacher and the child with whom the teacher was now working. If Tony persisted in doing this, then his feet were also tied so that he could not continue to interfere. Beyond that, he was totally ignored. The staff felt that it was vital not to reinforce his behavior by rewarding it with attention. As soon as the crying stopped and Tony was conpletely calm again, he was untied and immediately brought back to the task that had triggered the behavior. The rationale was that until Tony's enrollment at The Rimland School, his self-mutilative behavior and his tantrums had been the major weapon in his arsenal of resistance; and that, until now, had been a supremely effective means of task avoidance. At The Rimland School, it was no longer effective; he was required to perform the task anyway. Another area where we decided to attempt to effect a behavioral change was Tony's frequent trips to the toilet. A conversation with his mother and his pediatrician revealed that there was no physiological cause for his frequent urinating. On that basis, we no longer permitted Tony to run to the toilet as soon as a teacher started to work with him. Beyond that, we began to limit Tony's going to the toilet to once every half hour, then extended it to once every hour and so on.

Tony's evaluation in June, 1972, reports,

> There have been some major changes in Tony's behavior. He has become much more cooperative. At the outset, Tony averaged about five or six tantrums daily, some of them as long as 45 minutes in duration. Now he rarely has more than one or two a day, and these are usually very brief—five minutes or less. There are more and more days when he has none at all. He may go three successive days without needing to be placed in restraints. Very frequently now a verbal "no" from one of his teachers nips his self-destructive behavior in the bud. His physical attacks on his teachers occur much less frequently now. Even his other patterns of resistant behavior—the head turning, the hand wriggling, etc.—have become relatively rare.
>
> Tony now shows signs of pride in accomplishment. He has become more consistent, showing pleasure in his lessons and

abilities. He listens to simple directions and obeys commands. He no longer leaves the room at will, but tries to make his needs known and get teacher permission first. It has been a gradual process, but it appears that Tony has now adjusted to the realization that his resistant behavior will not release him from the completion of his assigned work. The result has been that Tony cooperates readily now for relatively long stretches of time just making happy sounds as he works. As for his frequent trips to the toilet, these have now ceased for the most part; in the main, he goes to the washroom only at the regularly scheduled intervals.

Performance-wise he has progressed in virtually every area. He is now able to match words, work correctly with sequential picture stories and indicate the correct answer from among a multiple choice grouping (the content of which has been read to him) when he is asked questions about character motivation, *et cetera,* relating to picture stories in his prereading workbook. He can sight-read some eleven words and so on. He responds to verbal commands, he does some independent seatwork in reading and math areas and completes independently some of the manual manipulative tasks he is given to do between his turns for individual tutoring. At both desk and chalkboard he responds correctly to commands like "Make a line going down" and "up." He can draw circles and crosses, and, with less control, he can trace triangles and squares. He is able to match the appropriate numeral to both concrete and pictured groupings, and is now learning problems involving concepts like $9 + 1$. He is much more cooperative in arts and crafts activities, an area over which we had to fight some major battles with him in the past; he's now able to do some cutting with scissors independently. He even stands still for the Pledge of Allegiance and the singing of America in the mornings, and has begun to participate without major resistance in the circle games and gross motor activities with the other children. Moreover, Tony now has a 15-word vocabulary and is able to combine some of these words into two-or-three-word phrases and/or short sentences. Tony is able to summon his newly-developed speech relatively readily in the speech therapy situation. In the classroom, however, it has thus far been difficult to elicit speech from him though we do succeed in getting him to imitate an occasional word or sound.

To sum up, the change in Tony in both behavioral and performance areas has been remarkable. We confidently expect that he will continue to progress during the coming school year.

Chapter VI

DISCUSSION AND CONCLUSIONS

EVEN IF THIS PAPER conveys nothing else, *the* one thing we want to be *sure* to communicate is this: The autistic child's atypical behavior and inadequate communicative abilities must not be the major determinant of the level of the educational program that is followed with the child. The immaturities and/or deficiencies in the child's general functioning—*including* the fact that the child may be nonverbal or noncommunicative—should never be used as an index of the likelihood of his being able to absorb and benefit from teaching at higher cognitive levels—specifically, his ability to learn reading, writing, and mathematics. With autistic children there may very well be a major discrepancy between the level at which the child proves able to perform in academic areas and the level at which he functions generally. The autistic child should *not* be denied his right to the intellectual stimulation that academic learnings may afford him simply because his spectrum of handicaps imprisons him behind a profoundly atypical facade.

Low teacher expectation in this regard is a self-fulfilling prophecy. We feel that it is crucial to emphasize this because too often no effort is made to teach autistic children, particularly the nonverbal autistic child, academic skills. Based on the child's atypical functioning and his frequently low IQ score (if a score is even obtainable), teachers and other professionals draw inferences that preclude their even *attempting* to teach the child anything as complex as, for example, reading. In two instances the anecdotal reports in the preceding chapter offer a case in point: the major contradictions between the 1970 and 1971 descriptions of Bill's conceptual capacities and of Don's in 1971 are striking when contrasted with both prior and subsequent reports of their abilities in academic areas. Such diametrically opposite findings can have stemmed

only from low teacher expectation (and perhaps teacher in-
adequacy in suitably adapting the teaching materials to allow
for their students' communicative deficiencies) coupled with
the children's typical initially-negative response to new instructors. Obviously, the teachers not only took no steps to
overcome this resistance, but they failed even to *recognize*
it as negativism. The failure here was the teachers', not the
children's. Multiplied by numerous similarly inadequate
teachers of autistic children in many other school programs
(whether analytically or behaviorally oriented), this adds up
to a criminal waste of possible human potential.

No cure has as yet been found for early childhood autism. In
the absence of a cure, appropriate remedial education, with
its promise of an improved level of functioning and the diminution of bizarre and abnormal behavior, together with the
accompanying hope that autistic children so taught will be
able to lead meaningful, even if perhaps sheltered, lives in
adulthood—remedial education offers the only viable alternative.

We have described the educational methods and techniques we have developed in our thirteen years of experience
in teaching and working with nonverbal and noncommunicative
autistic children. With adaptation when indicated, as we have
explained in preceding chapters, these methods are equally
valid for verbal autistic children. While our methods were
derived independently, their effectiveness is being confirmed
and substantiated by other researchers who have referred to
the use of similar approaches in the relatively recent literature.

For example, one of our basic precepts is the need to establish control at the very outset of the child's school attendance.
On this subject, Lorna Wing (1966) writes, ". . . screaming,
temper tantrums, destructiveness, aggressiveness and negativism can seriously interfere with the teaching process, and dealing with them cannot be deferred until the child can respond
to rational control" (p. 271–272). She suggests that immediate action be taken, "such as a smack, a loud firm 'no' or putting the child out of the room" (p. 272).

In Chapter IV, we wrote that at the beginning it would

almost certainly be necessary to repeatedly *re*-establish control, and that moreover, each new learning situation might result in still another battle of wills. In this connection, Dr. Wing (1966) asserts, ". . . autistic children can continue in a temper tantrum for many hours. However, they do respond to firm and consistent handling . . ." (p. 272). She goes on to emphasize the benefits of persistence on the adult's part: "Giving in merely prolongs the problem" (p. 273).

Basic to our approach is the idea that the teacher must intrude on the autistic child's detachment and withdrawal. In a recent paper, Rutter and Sussenwein (1971) write,

> It used to be thought that the autistic child *withdrew* from social contact due to anxiety and that, therefore, an attempt to interact before he is ready would only serve to increase his stress. Now that it is evident that rather than withdrawing from social contact he has failed to *develop* social contact, the opposite strategy is required. The adult must *intrude* on the child in order to deliberately engage him in interaction . . . (p. 380).

As we mentioned earlier, autistic children frequently resist learning a more complex skill than those which they have already been taught. We stressed the importance of the teacher's confronting and overcoming this resistance literally every single time it is encountered. About this, Lorna Wing (1966) maintains,

> . . . during the education of an autistic child, . . . the person who is trying to help him will be faced with the child's resistance to learning a new skill which the adult feels is important for the child and within his capacity. It is vital that the teacher . . . should win this struggle, not with any authoritarian aim, but in order to achieve a change in the child's attitude to learning which will eventually give him much greater independence (p. 273–274).

Another fundamental precept in our teaching approach is the manipulation of the child's limbs in order to teach him new skills kinesthetically, and thus bypass his difficulty in processing visual and auditory information. We have already cited Elgar's use of a similar method of teaching. In this same connection, Rutter and Sussenwein (1971) suggest "Free use must be made of gesture, demonstration and moving the child's hands or feet to show what is wanted" (p. 381).

We have stressed the necessity of limiting the child's autistic mannerisms during his lessons on the ground that these activities diminish the child's constructive output. Lovaas (1970) postulates a different reason for suppressing ritualistic behavior:

> . . . when the autistic child is engaged in self-stimulatory behavior, then he appears less responsive to auditory inputs. The self-stimulatory behavior apparently blocks his response to auditory signals. The . . . child can be trained to respond in spite of the self-stimulation, but this probably delays his acquisition of new behaviors (p. 34).

Though Lovaas attributes the child's reduced ability to learn while engaging in stereotyped mannerisms to a resultant blockage in the child's response to auditory stimuli, what is significant in the context of this paper is that Lovaas concurs with our belief that while this kind of behavior is in progress it inhibits the child's ability to learn and to perform a task.

A number of researchers have reported their findings relative to the autistic child's difficulties with language comprehension (J. K. Wing, 1966; Pronovost, *et al*, 1966; Rutter, 1968; Wing and Wing, 1971; Rutter and Bartak, 1971; Lorna Wing, 1972). However, we have seen no direct references in the literature to a somewhat-related phenomenon that we have observed: Some of the autistic children whom we have taught appear to have a problem in translating comprehension into motor performance. For example, Don, one of the seven children described in the preceding chapter, is a case in point. During his lesson periods, Don's written replies to questions seem to indicate excellent comprehension. On the *performance* level, however, his comprehension appears to be much less consistent. In terms of performance, he shows evidence of a deficiency in comprehension. On one occasion we discussed this with Don. The following is a verbatim transcription of Don's written replies to the oral questions we put to him. He was at that time ten years old, and still completely nonverbal.

Q. How come you didn't do what I asked you to? Didn't you understand, or what?

A. I don't know what the trouble is, really, not understanding or the fact that somehow I'm not ever sure that I'm right.

Q. How do you mean, 'not sure you're right?'

A. Not sure that I'm understanding what means what. Meanings of words have always mixed me up.

Q. I'm talking to you in words *now.* Are you mixed up about the meaning of what I'm saying?

A. No.

Q. Well, then—in what situations *do* words mix you up, then?

A. They mix me up in situations where when the need to think interrupts the thing that needs to be done.

The nearest we can come to an interpretation of this problem is that it seems to represent a kind of "I can't think when I'm in motion" situation.

A more recent incident in which Don was involved further illustrates this seeming inability to translate comprehension into motor performance. At the time of this occurrence, Don was fourteen and one-half years old. At school one day, he participated with the other children in a group game, A Tisket, A Tasket. The rules of the game had been carefully explained to everyone beforehand. Nevertheless, when the beanbag was dropped behind Don and it was his turn to chase the other player around the circle, it became obvious that he was genuinely confused about just what he was supposed to do. This, despite the preceding explanation and the fact that he had already seen some five or six of his schoolmates play the game correctly. Subsequently, when we returned to the classroom, we asked Don to explain the game. (Though Don had developed speech by this time, it was grossly inadequate, and on this occasion, too, he communicated with us in writing.) Don was able to write out an accurate, sequential description of how the game should be played. Yet, despite this seeming comprehension, in a veridical situation he had been unable to *do* it! We do not consider Don's written explanation of the game here to be an example of the "closed loop" phenomenon in autistic children (where the child repeats what he has previously heard verbatim, with no evidence of comprehension) referred to by Pronovost (1966), Rimland (1964), and others, because Don's version of the game was written in his own words.

The only reference we have seen in the literature which might apply indirectly to this problem of comprehension versus performance, is this comment by Hermelin (1966):

> This is an experiment which directly investigated "what is it" compared to "where is it" discrimination. We used four upturned aluminum boxes of different lengths, and subsequently four boxes of the same length . . . In the first part of the experiment the children had to select either a box which could vary in length but whose position in the series was constant, or a box whose position varied but which always had a certain length. Thus the two tasks each had one positive dimension, which was the rewarded feature, either position or length, and one negative one, which had to be disregarded, i.e., either length or position. When the child lifted the correct box out of the four in front of him, he found a sweet underneath it. The results of this first experiment were that normal as well as autistic children learned much quicker to discriminate according to place than to length . . . many more autistics and normals did not learn the length discrimination over the same number of trials. This result confirms . . . the experiment where a motor movement to a particular place was learned far more readily than a visual discrimination, where the direction of the movement had to vary with the input. Thus varying input with constant output was easier than constant input with varying output (p. 169).

Interestingly, there is a comment by Fred's therapist as reported in the case study material in the preceding chapter which also touches on this problem: "Receptive speech is quite good," the report reads. "Fred seems to understand nearly everything that is said to him and ordinarily responds in an appropriate fashion. Response breakdown occurs when the communication includes a request for some bodily action. He seems to have difficulty translating word input into muscle output and such output usually must be gesturally demonstrated before it is accomplished the first time."

It would seem that research in this area—the problem of translating comprehension into motor performance—might provide some fruitful information about the specific language deficits of some autistic children.

Elgar (1966) refers to "the characteristic dyslexic difficulty with letters that are differentiated on direction alone—b, d; p, q . . . etc." (p. 219). Although our children have some major problems with writing, we have not encountered a problem with reversals *per se* with our youngsters. What we *have* encountered is similar to what Elgar then describes further: "Often a child trying to write, say, the letter 'b' will put it upside down or horizontally instead of vertically. Oblique strokes may present special difficulty—'A' being written 'H', for example" (pp. 219–220). Because we teach our children cursive writing from the outset rather than manuscript printing, our children don't evince this difficulty in precisely the form that Elgar describes but they do exhibit similar problems. However, unlike Elgar, we don't attribute these difficulties to dyslexia, which implies a problem in the child's initial *perception* of the directionality of the letter. We believe that this is entirely a problem in *execution*—apraxia, rather than dyslexia.

There is one other area related to, but not identical with, the precept with which we opened this chapter. We want to discuss it here, briefly. Our experience with autistic children has taught us that, as a general rule, they almost never display spontaneously so much as a thimbleful of higher level capability and performance than one asks of them. The child may be *capable* of doing work at a more advanced level, but if he is asked to perform at a lower level, *that* level is where he does perform—and not always necessarily even with consistent accuracy—without revealing in any way that he can actually deal proficiently with much more difficult work. For this reason, it is extremely important that his teacher try to lead the autistic child into higher levels of cognitive performance than his general functioning would seem to indicate is appropriate. As a case in point: When we read Hewett's report of the successful outcome of his efforts to teach reading and writing to Jimmy, the 13-year-old nonverbal autistic boy described in

Chapter II of this book, we were struck by the fact that nowhere in the story is there any mention of giving the child an opportunity to compose sentences dealing with something other than just his wants and needs, and thus perhaps expressing his own inner thoughts and ideas. The obvious inference seems to be that conceptualization at that level was beyond Jimmy's capabilities. And maybe it was. However, as a rule, children like Jimmy exhibit a major deficit in their ability to initiate new behaviors. Unless they are encouraged to formulate their own thoughts by being asked, say, a "what" or better still, a "why" question to answer in writing, there is very little likelihood that they will demonstrate their ability to do so. It's regrettable that apparently there was no effort made to find out whether Jimmy was, in fact, capable of it. In our own situation, our outward display of confident expectancy as we ask for a level of performance that we are sometimes inwardly certain is beyond a particular child's intellectual development, has, more frequently than not, been positively and astoundingly rewarded! And what is more important is that the child's motivation and enjoyment seem to increase as the work presented to him becomes more challenging.

If we seem to be placing undue emphasis on the importance of academic work for autistic children, and especially nonverbal autistic children, it is only because, as we mentioned earlier, so frequently in their school experience these children are judged on the basis of their atypical functioning with the automatic accompanying inference that academic achievement is beyond their cognitive capabilities. This is, of course, as we said at the outset of this chapter, a self-fulfilling prophecy. Sybil Elgar (1966) makes the point that there is no need to wait for a learning block "to be overcome before introducing ordinary formal education" (p. 211). She continues,

> . . . as their disturbed behavior lessens, so the opportunity specifically to teach the child presents itself. The non-directive approach, at this stage, must be condemned. Not to attempt remedial teaching is equivalent to refusing to teach a deaf child to lip-read. Nothing, to my mind, is more tragic than to see a child who is ready to make progress in achieving understanding

of the world, being given the equivalent of "diversionary occupational therapy" in the misguided belief that this will, in
time, bring out his supposedly unimpaired learning capacities
(pp. 217–218).

We believe very strongly that no one has the right to play
God by attempting to prejudge any child's cognitive potential.
Certainly, in every instance, there should be a sustained and
persistent effort to develop *every* area of the autistic child's
functioning: his motor performance, socialization skills, social
awareness, *et cetera*, as well as his academic abilities. Even
if it should subsequently develop that his academic learnings have no functional utility in the sense that he
does not employ these learnings volitionally, the effort that
goes into the teaching and the learning is a worthwhile endeavor because it contributes to the storehouse of knowledge
from which the autistic child builds his world, and from which
the autistic adult derives a world.

With reference to the older autistic child, Rutter (1966b)
writes,

> Although it is unusual, but not unknown, for a marked im-
> provement to begin for the first time in late childhood or
> adolescence, it is *frequent* for improvement, learning and acquisi-
> tion of skills to continue well into adult life. Although probably
> adequate schooling should begin early to be most effective . . .
> certainly no age can be laid down when it is "too late" (p. 99).

So there is much that still needs to be done in terms of remedial education for all autistic children, and particularly
for nonverbal and noncommunicative autistic children. There
is a need to develop effective methods of vocational training.
There is a need to develop modified sheltered workshops for
those autistics who remain nonverbal into adulthood, and whose
functioning continues to be so atypical that they would not be
acceptable even in the traditional sheltered workshop. For
some, in Benson's words (1972), "it seems at this time too much
to hope that . . . they will ever be able to live a fully independent life in society. Unless, of course, there should be a dra-
matic breakthrough in our knowledge of" autism, its causes
and its treatment (p. 28). And for these autistic adults there

is a need to start thinking in terms of developing residential communities where, Benson continues,

> . . . it would seem essential to make provision for a continuation of the type of remedial education which has proved so beneficial. . . . Such education should be available far beyond the normal school-leaving age. . . . indeed, for as long as the individual can benefit from it.
>
> In parallel with continued schooling, training in such activities as suit his temperament and abilities will be needed; for example, craft work, horticulture, and a variety of manual tasks (p. 29).

In response to those who argue that setting up a residential community solely for autistic people is ill-advised, Dr. Benson replies, as *we* would to a similar argument,

> . . . perhaps it would . . . be far better to develop facilities like this for a multiplicity of handicaps, all together under one umbrella. . . . However, I see two basic requirements for autistic members of a special community. Firstly, there should be no exclusion because an individual is particularly 'difficult'. . . . This can lead to the exclusion of the very people who most need help, and . . . our communities must be flexible enough to cope. Secondly, any association with other forms of handicap must recognise at all times the special needs of autistic persons, and any attempt to make them conform to unsuitable conditions, in the name of convenience, would be unacceptable (p. 29).

From such a community, those who are capable of it can go out daily to their work in competitive employment; and the others can be productive, each according to his own abilities, within the community itself. Thus the community residents would contribute to its financing, and with long range planning for learning, work and recreation and leisure-time activities, the residents would be assured of happy and meaningful lives.

Chapter VII

SUMMARY

IN THE YEARS immediately following Kanner's delineation of the syndrome early infantile autism in 1943, the belief was widespread that autism is an emotional illness, and that there could be no attempt at educating autistic children until after successful psychotherapeutic treatment had been effected. In actual fact, however, most autistic children were receiving neither treatment nor education.

By the middle of the 1960's, a growing number of researchers began to believe that autism might stem from other than emotional causes, and in the past seven or eight years, a considerable body of literature has appeared in the professional journals relative to the results of research into educational methods and approaches.

This book holds to the organic theory of causation. We have described the handicaps of autistic children and outlined a behaviorally-oriented educational approach within a developmental framework which we have developed during the past 13 years of teaching and working with nonverbal, noncommunicative and verbal autistic children. We have also presented supporting case studies and anecdotal reports, and have reviewed the work of some of the researchers whose findings seem to confirm the validity of our methods. In addition, we have suggested an area of autistic functioning which may hold promise for future research, and have outlined briefly some of the work that remains to be done in planning for the future of autistic adults.

REFERENCES

1. Arnold, G. E.: Writing instead of speaking. *Curr. Probl. Phoniat. Logoped., 1:* 155–162, 1960.
2. Baranyay, E. P.: *The Mentally Handicapped Adolescent, The Slough Project of the National Society for Mentally Handicapped Children.* Oxford, Pergamon Press, 1971.
3. Benson, G. K.: Communities—and hope for the future. *10th Anniversary, National Society for Autistic Children, June, 1972 Communication.* 28–29, 1972.
4. Bettelheim, B.: *The Empty Fortress.* New York, The Free Press, 1967.
5. Churchill, D. W.: The relation of infantile autism and early childhood schizophrenia to developmental language disorders of childhood. *Journal of Autism and Childhood Schizophrenia, 2*(2) : 182–197, 1972.
6. Clark, G. D.: An Education Programme for Psychotic Children. In Weston, P.T.B. (Ed.) *Some Approaches to Teaching Autistic Children, A Collection of Papers.* Oxford, Pergamon Press, 1965.
7. Collection of Papers. Appendix I—Terminology. In *Collection of Papers Deriving from the Course of Lectures on the Education of Autistic Children Held at the Society School for Autistic Children in Autumn, 1967.* (Mimeo). London, The National Society for Autistic Children, 1967.
8. Cowan, L. and Goldman, M.: The selection of the mentally deficient for vocational training and the effect of this training on vocational success. In Stahlecker, L. V. (Ed.) *Occupational Information for the Mentally Retarded.* Springfield, Charles C Thomas, 1967.
9. DesLauriers, A. M. and Carlson, C. F.: *Your Child Is Asleep.* Homewood, The Dorsey Press, 1969.
10. Despert, J. L.: Foreword. In Wing, L. *Autistic Children.* New York, Brunner/Mazel, 1972.
11. Doernberg, N., Rosen, B., and Walker, T. T.: *A Home Training Program for Young Mentally Ill Children.* Brooklyn, League School for Seriously Disturbed Children, 1968.
12. Eisenberg, L. and Kanner, L.: Early infantile autism, 1943–1955. *American Journal of Orthopsychiatry, 26* (July) : 556–566, 1956.
13. Elgar, S.: Teaching Autistic Children. In Wing, J. K. (Ed.) *Early*

Childhood Autism, Clinical, Educational and Social Aspects.
Oxford, Pergamon Press, 205–237, 1966.

14. Elgar, S.: Specific Teaching. In *Collection of Papers Deriving
from the Course of Lectures on the Education of Autistic
Children Held at the Society School for Autistic Children in
Autumn, 1967.* (Mimeo). London, The National Society for
Autistic Children, 37–40, 1968.

15. Fenichel, Carl: Psycho-educational approaches for seriously disturbed children in the classroom. In *Intervention Approaches in
Educating Emotionally Disturbed Children.* Syracuse, Division
of Special Education and Rehabilitation, Syracuse University,
1966.

16. Fenichel, C., Freedman, A. M., and Klapper, Z.: A day school
for schizophrenic children. *American Journal of Orthopsychiatry, 30*(1): 130–143, 1960.

17. Ferster, C. B.: Positive reinforcement and behavioral deficits of
autistic children. *Child Development, 32:* 437–456, 1961.

18. Ferster, C. B.: The repertoire of the autistic child in relation
to principles of reinforcement. In Gottschalk, L. and Auerbach,
A. H. (Eds.) *Methods of Research in Psychotherapy.* New
York, Appleton-Century-Crofts, 1966.

19. Goodwin, M. S., Cowen, M. A., and Goodwin, T. C.: Malabsorp-
tion and cerebral dysfunction: a multivariate and comparative
study of autistic children. *Journal of Autism and Childhood
Schizophrenia, 1*(1): 48–62, 1971.

20. Goodwin, M. S., and Goodwin, T. C.: In a dark mirror. *Mental
Hygiene, 53*(4): 550–563, 1969.

21. Hermelin, Beate: Psychological Research. In Wing, J. K. (Ed.)
*Early Childhood Autism, Clinical, Educational and Social As-
pects.* Oxford, Pergamon Press, 159–174, 1966.

22. Hewett, F. M.: Teaching reading to an autistic boy through operant
conditioning. *Reading Teacher, 17,* 613–618, 1964.

23. Hewett, F. M.: Teaching speech to an autistic child through
operant conditioning. *American Journal of Orthopsychiatry,
35*(5), 927–936, 1965.

24. Hewett, F. M.: The autistic child as teacher and learner. In
Park, C. C. (Ed.) *Research and Education: Top Priorities for
Mentally Ill Children. Proceedings of the 2nd Annual Meeting
and Conference of the National Society for Autistic Children,
June 24–27, 1970.* Public Health Service Publication No.
2164, 51–55.

25. Hewett, F. M., Mayhew, D., and Rabb, E.: An experimental reading program for neurologically impaired, mentally retarded, and
severely emotionally disturbed children. *American Journal of
Orthopsychiatry, 37:* 35–48, 1967.

26. Himwich, H. E., Jenkins, R. L., Fujimori, M., Narasimhachari, N., and Ebersole, M.: A biochemical study of early infantile autism. *Journal of Autism and Childhood Schizophrenia, 2*(2):114–126, 1972.

27. Hingtgen, J. N., Coulter, S. K., and Churchill, D. W.: Intensive reinforcement of imitative behavior in mute autistic children. *Archives of General Psychiatry, 17* (July): 36–43, 1967, Copyright 1967, American Medical Association.

28. Hingtgen, J. N., Sanders, B. J., and DeMyer, M. K.: Shaping Cooperative Responses in Early Childhood Schizophrenics. In Ullman, L. and Krasner, L. (Eds.) *Case Studies in Behavior Modification.* New York, Holt, Rinehart, and Winston, 1965.

29. Jensen, G. D. and Womack, M. G.: Operant conditioning techniques applied in the treatment of an autistic child. *American Journal of Orthopsychiatry, 37,* 30–34, 1967.

30. Kanner, L.: Autistic disturbances of affective contact. *Nervous Child, 2*(3): 217–250, 1943.

31. Kanner, L.: Early infantile autism. *The Journal of Pediatrics, 25*(3), 211–217, 1944.

32. Kanner, L.: Problems of nosology and psychodynamics of early infantile autism. *American Journal of Orthopsychiatry, 19*(3), 416–426, 1949.

33. Kanner, L.: *Child Psychiatry,* 3rd Edition. Springfield, Charles C Thomas, 1957.

34. Kanner, L.: Follow-up study of eleven autistic children originally reported in 1943. *Journal of Autism and Childhood Schizophrenia, 1*(2): 119–145, 1971.

35. Kanner, L. and Eisenberg, L.: Notes on the Follow-Up Studies of Autistic Children. In Hoch, P. H. and Zubin, J. (Eds.) *Psychopathology of Childhood.* New York, Grune & Stratton, 1955, 227–239.

36. Kanner, L. and Lesser, L. I.: Early infantile autism. *Pediatric Clinics of North America, 5*(3), 711–730, 1958.

37. Kephart, N. C.: *The Slow Learner in the Classroom.* Columbus, Charles E. Merrill, 1960.

38. Kolstoe, O. P.: An Examination of Some Characteristics Which Discriminate Between Employed and Not-Employed Mentally Retarded Males. In Stahlecker, L. V. (Ed.) *Occupational Information for the Mentally Retarded.* Springfield, Charles C Thomas, 48–65, 1967.

39. Kvaraceus, W. C., and Hayes, E. N.: (Eds.) *If Your Child is Handicapped.* Boston, Porter Sargent, 327–339, 1969.

40. Lovaas, O. I.: A Program for the Establishment of Speech in Psychotic Children. In Wing, J. K. (Ed.) *Early Childhood Autism, Clinical, Educational and Social Aspects.* Oxford, Pergamon Press, 115–144, 1966a.

41. Lovaas, O. I.: Learning theory approach to the treatment of childhood schizophrenia. Paper presented at Symposium on Childhood Schizophrenia, *American Orthopsychiatric Association,* San Francisco, 1966b.
42. Lovaas, O. I.: Strengths and weaknesses of operant conditioning techniques for the treatment of autism. In Park, C. C. (Ed.) *Research and Education: Top Priorities for Mentally Ill Children. Proceedings of the 2nd Annual Meeting and Conference of the National Society for Autistic Children, June 24-27, 1970.* Public Health Service Publication No. 2164, 30-41.
43. Lovaas, O. I., Berberich, J. P., Perloff, B. F. and Schaeffer, B.: Acquisition of imitative speech by schizophrenic children. *Science, 151,* 3711 (Feb. 11): 705-707, 1966a.
44. Lovaas, O. I., *et al.:* Establishment of social reinforcers in two schizophrenic children on the basis of food. *Journal of Experimental Child Psychology, 4* (Oct.): 109-125, 1966b.
45. Lovaas, O. I., Schreibman, L., Koegel, R., and Rehm, R.: Selective responding by autistic children to multiple sensory input. *Journal of Abnormal Psychology, 77*(3): 211-222, 1971.
46. Mittler, P.: Psychological Assessment. In Wing, J. K. (Ed.) *Early Childhood Autism, Clinical, Educational and Social Aspects.* Oxford, Pergamon Press, 145-158, 1966.
47. Moore, D. J., and Shiek, D. A.: Toward a theory of early infantile autism. *Psychological Review, 78:* 451-456, 1971.
48. Ney, P. G., Palvesky, E., and Markely, J.: Relative effectiveness of operant conditioning and play therapy in childhood schizophrenia. *Journal of Autism and Childhood Schizophrenia, 1*(3): 337-349, 1971.
49. Oppenheim, R. C.: They said our child was hopeless. *Saturday Evening Post, 23:* 56-58, June 17, 1961.
50. Park, C. C.: *The Siege.* New York, Harcourt, Brace & World, 1967.
51. Pribram, K.: Autism: a deficiency in context-dependent processes? In Park, C. C. (Ed.) *Research and Education: Top Priorities for Mentally Ill Children. Proceedings of the 2nd Annual Meeting and Conference of the National Society for Autistic Children, June 24-27, 1970.* Public Health Service Publication No. 2164, 42-50.
52. Pronovost, W., Wakstein, M. P., and Wakstein, D. J.: A longitudinal study of the speech behavior and language comprehension of fourteen children diagnosed atypical or autistic. *Exceptional Children, 33:* 19-26, 1966.
53. Rimland, B.: *Infantile Autism. The Syndrome and Its Implications for a Neural Theory of Behavior.* New York, Appleton-Century-Crofts, 1964.

54. Risley, T. and Wolf, M.: Establishing functional speech in echolalic children. *Behavior Research and Therapy, 5:* 73–88, 1967.

55. Ritvo, E. R., Yuwiler, A., Geller, E., Kales, A., Rashkis, S., Schicor, A., Plotkin, S., Axelrod, R., and Howard, C.: Effects of L-dopa in autism. *Journal of Autism and Childhood Schizophrenia, 1*(2): 190–205, 1971.

56. Rutter, M.: Behavioral and Cognitive Characteristics of a Series of Psychotic Children. In Wing, J. K. (Ed.) *Early Childhood Autism, Clinical, Educational and Social Aspects.* Oxford, Pergamon Press, 51–81, 1966a.

57. Rutter, M.: Prognosis: Psychotic Children in Adolescence and Early Adult Life. In Wing, J. K. (Ed.) *Early Childhood Autism, Clinical, Educational and Social Aspects.* Oxford, Pergamon Press, 83–99, 1966b.

58. Rutter, M.: Concepts of autism: a review of research. *Journal of Child Psychology and Psychiatry, 9:* 1–25, 1968.

59. Rutter, M. L. and Bartak, L.: Causes of infantile autism: some considerations from recent literature. *Journal of Autism and Childhood Schizophrenia, 1*(1):20–32, 1971.

60. Rutter, M. and Sussenwein, F.: A developmental and behavioral approach to the treatment of preschool autistic children. *Journal of Autism and Childhood Schizophrenia, 1*(4): 376–397, 1971.

61. Sapon, S.: Establishing verbal behavior in speech-handicapped children. In Park, C. C. (Ed.) *Proceedings of the 4th Annual Meeting and Conference of the National Society for Autistic Children, June 21–24, 1972.* In press.

62. Schopler, E. and Reichler, R. J.: Parents as cotherapists in the treatment of psychotic children. *Journal of Autism and Childhood Schizophrenia, 1*(1): 87–102, 1971.

63. Taft, L. T. and Cohen, H. J.: Hypsarrythmia and infantile autism: a clinical report. *Journal of Autism and Childhood Schizophrenia, 1*(3): 327–336, 1971.

64. Tobias, J. and Gorelick, J.: Work Characteristics of Retarded Adults at Trainable Levels. In Stahlecker, L. V. (Ed.) *Occupational Information for the Mentally Retarded.* Springfield, Charles C Thomas, 189–197, 1967.

65. Wilson, M. D.: Problems in Providing Special Education. In Wing, J. K. (Ed.) *Early Childhood Autism, Clinical, Educational and Social Aspects.* Oxford, Pergamon Press, 175–183, 1966.

66. Wilson, M.: Autistic Children in the Classroom. In *Collection of Papers Deriving from the Course of Lectures on the Education of Autistic Children Held at the Society School for Au-*

tistic Children in Autumn, 1967. (Mimeo). London, The National Society for Autistic Children, 30–36, 1968.

67. Wing, J. K.: Foreword. In Wing, J. K. (Ed.) *Early Childhood Autism, Clinical, Educational and Social Aspects.* Oxford, Pergamon Press, xi–xiii, 1966.

68. Wing, J. K.: Diagnosis, Epidemiology, Aetiology. In Wing, J. K. (Ed.) *Early Childhood Autism, Clinical, Educational and Social Aspects.* Oxford, Pergamon Press, 3–49, 1966.

69. Wing, J. K.: Book Reviews: The Empty Fortress by Bruno Bettelheim. *British Journal of Psychiatry,* 114, 789–791, 1968.

70. Wing, Lorna: Counselling and the Principles of Management. In Wing, J. K. (Ed.) *Early Childhood Autism, Clinical, Educational and Social Aspects.* Oxford, Pergamon Press, 257–277, 1966.

71. Wing, Lorna: Diagnosis of Autism and Handicaps of Autistic Children. In *Collection of Papers Deriving from the Course of Lectures on the Education of Autistic Children Held at the Society School for Autistic Children in Autumn, 1967.* (Mimeo). London, The National Society for Autistic Children, 6–13, 1968.

72. Wing, Lorna: *Autistic Children, A Guide for Parents and Professionals.* New York, Brunner/Mazel, 1972.

73. Wing, J. K. and Wing, L.: A Clinical Interpretation of Remedial Teaching. In Wing, J. K. (Ed.) *Early Childhood Autism, Clinical, Educational and Social Aspects.* Oxford, Pergamon Press, 185–204, 1966.

74. Wing, L. and Wing, J. K.: Multiple impairments in early childhood autism. *Journal of Autism and Childhood Schizophrenia, 1*(3): 256–266, 1971.

INDEX

A

Ability
  imitative, 39
    (*see also* Behavior, imitative and
    Imitative behavior)
Abnormal behaviors, 40
    (*see also* Autistic children, be-
    havioral abnormalities of
    and Behavior, abnormalities
    of)
Academic skills
  teaching of, 51
    (*see also* Teaching academic
    skills)
Adapting
  materials, 51
  methods, 51
  techniques, 51
  to children's individual disabilities,
    51
Adolescents
  autistic, 42
  teachability of, 42
    (*see also* Autistic child, older)
Adulthood
  autistic children in, 62, 91
Affection
  gestures of, 42, 44
Aggressiveness, 91
    (*see also* Behavior, aggressive)
Allocation of teaching time, 43
Analytically-oriented program, 91
Approval, 41–42
Apraxia, 96
Arithmetic
  teaching of, 44, 55, 58
Arnold, G. E., 9, 10
Arts and crafts
  teaching of, 45, 57
Assessment
  of strengths and weaknesses, 32
Assistance
  fading of, 39–40

Attend
  need for child to, 34, 40
Attending to task and teacher
  how accomplished, 40–41
Attitude of teachers, 36, 61
  to learning, 92
Atypical behavior(s), 40, 90
  diminution of, 91
Auditory
  discrimination, 51–52
  inputs, 93
  teaching, 38
Autism
  behavioral characteristics of, 3, 28,
    29
  biological hypothesis of, 26
  causes of, 25
  early infantile, 3, 6
  etiology of, 25
  incidence of, 4, 25
  psychogenic hypothesis of, 6, 7,
    20, 25
  sensory and affective deprivation
    in, 19
  sex ratio in, 4
  symptoms of, 3, 37
    (*see also* Autistic children)
Autistic adults, 100
Autistic child
  older, 98
Autistic children
  anecdotal reports, 63–89
  behavioral abnormalities of, 28–29,
    31
    (*see also* Abnormal behaviors)
  capacities of, 8, 32
  characteristics of, 3, 28–29
  cognitive potentialities of, 3, 98
  deficiencies of, 27–32, 33
  description of, 27–29
  difficulty in testing of, 32, 33
  disabilities of, 27–32
  echolalic, 47

educability of nonverbal, 6, 42
handicaps of, 25–33
inaccessibility of, 6, 7
incidence of nonverbal, 28
intelligence of, 3, 4
nonverbal, 6, 8, 9, 11, 14, 21, 47,
    90, 98
psychiatric treatment of, 7
retesting of, 32, 33
social maturity of, 45
speaking, 8, 11, 61
teachability of, in adolescence, 42
ultimate employability of, 45
untestability of, 33
verbal, 8, 11, 14, 61
Autistic mannerisms, 40, 93
Autistic rituals, 44
Avoidance of tasks, 37

B

Ball
  bouncing, catching, throwing, 56
Baronyay, E. P., 45
Bartak, L., 4, 30, 93
Base-line estimate, 33
Battles of will, 34, 37
  (*see also* Struggles for power)
Behavior
  abnormalities of, 28–29, 31
  aggressive, 15, 37
    (*see also* Aggressiveness)
  bizarre, 3, 61
    (*see also* Bizarre behaviors)
  confronting unacceptable, 61, 92
  extinguishing undesirable, 22, 61
  imitative, 14, 15, 21, 22, 55, 56, 57
  self-destructive, 36
  self-stimulatory, 93
  shaping of, 15
  social, promoting, 45, 55
  tantrum, 15, 61
    (*see also* Behaviors)
Behavior modification techniques, 11,
    15
Behavior therapy, 11, 15
Behavioral
  abnormalities, 28–29, 31
    (*see also* Abnormal behaviors)

anomalies, 28–29
characteristics, 3
management, 59
repertoire, 14, 61
strategies, 61
Behaviorally-oriented program, 61,
    91
Behaviors
  atypical, 40, 90
  teaching new, 22
    (*see also* Behavior)
Benson, G. K., 98–99
Bettelheim, B., 21, 23, 25
Biological hypothesis, 26
Biological theory of causation, 26
Bizarre behavior(s), 61
  diminution of, 91
  during work sessions, 40
    (*see also* Behavior, bizarre)
Bizarre mannerisms
  prevention of, 40
Body image concepts, 45, 46

C

Capacities
  of autistic children, 8, 32
Carlson, C. F., 19, 20, 21
Causes of autism, 25
Central vision, 41, 57
Characteristics
  of autistic children, 3, 28–29
  of teachers, 60, 61
Child and teacher
  interaction between, 46
  relationship between, 46
Childhood schizophrenias, 6
Child-teacher ratio, 43
Churchill, D. W., 14, 21, 31, 54
Clark, G. D., 23
Class size, 43
"Closed loop" phenomenon, 95
Cognitive
  abilities, 8
  potential, 3, 98
Cohen, H. J., 26
Collection of Papers, 30
Commands to children
  giving of, 48